I0114951

The Rise and Fall of Modern Man

MODERNITY IN QUESTION
STUDIES IN PHILOSOPHY AND HISTORY OF IDEAS

Edited by Małgorzata Kowalska

VOLUME 9

PETER LANG
EDITION

Jacek Dobrowolski

The Rise and Fall of Modern Man
Translated by Simon Loeb and Joanna Guzowska

PETER LANG
EDITION

Bibliographic Information published by the Deutsche Nationalbibliothek
The Deutsche Nationalbibliothek lists this publication in the
Deutsche Nationalbibliografie; detailed bibliographic data is available in the
internet at http://dnb.d-nb.de.

Library of Congress Cataloging-in-Publication Data
Names: Dobrowolski, Jacek, 1976- author.
Title: The rise and fall of modern man / Jacek Dobrowolski.
Description: New York : Peter Lang, 2017. | Series: Modernity in question,
ISSN 2193-3421 ; Vol. 9 | Includes bibliographical references.
Identifiers: LCCN 2016056961 | ISBN 9783631712689
Subjects: LCSH: Philosophical anthropology. | Human beings--History.
Classification: LCC BD450 .D625 2017 | DDC 128--dc23 LC record available at
https://lccn.loc.gov/2016056961

This publication was financially supported by the University of Warsaw.

Jacek Dobrowolski's Essay *The Rise and Fall of Modern Man* was awarded
an honorable mention in the second edition of the Barbara Skarga Essay Contest
announced by the *Foundation for Thought* in May 2013. The result was announced
in October 2014. The essay answers the question:
Can science and technology answer the ancient challenge: Know Thyself?

Cover image: Courtesy of Grazyna Smalej

ISSN 2193-3421
ISBN 978-3-631-71268-9 (Print)
E-ISBN 978-3-631-71303-7 (E-PDF)
E-ISBN 978-3-631-71304-4 (EPUB)
E-ISBN 978-3-631-71305-1 (MOBI)
DOI 10.3726/b10822

© Peter Lang GmbH
Internationaler Verlag der Wissenschaften
Frankfurt am Main 2017
All rights reserved.
Peter Lang Edition is an Imprint of Peter Lang GmbH.

Peter Lang – Frankfurt am Main · Bern · Bruxelles · New York ·
Oxford · Warszawa · Wien

All parts of this publication are protected by copyright. Any
utilisation outside the strict limits of the copyright law, without
the permission of the publisher, is forbidden and liable to
prosecution. This applies in particular to reproductions,
translations, microfilming, and storage and processing in
electronic retrieval systems.

This publication has been peer reviewed.

www.peterlang.com

Table of Contents

1. Introduction: Who, Whom, Why and How?

There are two responses to the question of whether science and technology can answer the ancient challenge Know Thyself and both of them are "no". The first of these negative responses is rather trivial: they cannot because only the self-knowing-self can answer this challenge or not. Only the knowing self. Science and technology can merely assist, hinder or perhaps be neutral in this task, "adding up to zero", bringing into it as many pluses as minuses. But can science and technology play this role at all? Could "self-knowledge" ever be one of their goals? Even if the final cause of the existence of science and technology—if there is one, and one can reasonably doubt that there is—has anything to do with the ancient commercial slogan of Pythia, it is that the first turn from "knowledge of nature" to "self-knowledge" in the history of Western thought, the Socratic turn, took place under the patronage and as part of the transfer of this slogan from the sacred space of the Oracle to the space of Philosophy. From its very inception Western science and its product in the form of technology followed a different course: the knowledge of what is objective, or nature, as opposed to the course of subjectivity, or what is human. In the very roots of our thinking, which would be difficult to cut off or uproot, there lies a difference between these two, a difference stemming from the perhaps most fundamental dualism of "subject" and "object". Science, and even more so technology, lack the means to transcend this dualism which precedes them, and they do not have the need to do so.

However, going beyond the triviality of this straightforward remark we assume that the question in fact refers to that "someone" and their self-knowledge as well as to how science and technology, regardless of their own destiny, can be useful to that someone in the task of self-knowing, and, in a slightly different sense, to how the nomothetical sciences and their accompanying technological development impact the ideographic sciences, the humanities. Following this assumption, after a long and winding course, we will arrive at the second "no" which is complex, ambiguous and mediated by a variety of always partial "yes" and "insofar as". It will in fact be a kind of "rather not, although…", which again may seem trivial but, as is usually the case, the pearls lie in the details. Therefore, without feigned embarrassment about the triviality of the point of arrival, let us walk the stages of the road I have sketched in this essay whose main variables will be the "who" and "what" implicit in the titular challenge.

Know Thyself. Know the Ego. This someone, the knowing subject as we have referred to him before, although perhaps prematurely, is undoubtedly a construct and not something out there, simply given. In the course of this essay and the dynamics of its discourse he will be construed and re-construed, far removed from any "naturalness" or immediacy and yet with pretense to a kind of "factual truth" or authenticity. However, this truth or authenticity can only be granted to him through such "categories" as human, person, subject, the I, individual, being, author etc. all of which are highly suspect, always controversial and ultimately groundless, imploding in the ecstasy and divergence of their meanings and subject to numerous crushing deconstructions. Each determination of this someone who is referred to in the essay question will be a choice which has to exclude or ignore something and exaggerate beyond proper measure something else, introducing some deformation—but of what? Of this unknown something, allegedly identical with the one who knows himself, something so complex but at the same time most intimate that it cannot be easily removed, circumvented, forgotten or distanced, even if there is good reason to doubt its reality. We should also remember that not only human individuals can be subjects. The subject may also be God, other spirits, collectives (classes, nations, religious communities, minorities, corporations etc.) and abstract concepts: man as such, modern man, John Doe etc. All of these subjects can turn out to be the addressees of the challenge Know Thyself.

Let us capture the problem with a list. The ancient challenge that we are considering can be directed at:

(a) Man knowing his nature.
(b) The soul knowing its spirituality or divinity.
(c) An individual knowing their individuality.
(d) A human person knowing their personhood and personality.
(e) The cognitive subject knowing their subjectivity.
(f) The absolute spirit knowing itself, that is, the totality of what there is.

(g) A thinking animal knowing its life/body.

(h) A class knowing itself as such and becoming a class for itself.

(i) Any data processing entity processing data regarding itself.

(j) The author of this essay knowing himself through self-contemplation.

This is what the Western philosophical tradition suggests most readily and several other variants can certainly be added. What is interesting is that these options are not mutually exclusive or clearly demarcated, just as individuality is not clearly distinguished from spirituality or corporeality. Perhaps only considering all of them and applying them interchangeably can lead to a relatively exhaustive answer to the proposed question in the spirit of, respectively: (a) humanism, (b) anthropo-theology of Socratic-Platonic provenance, (c) individualism, (d) personalism, (e) subjectivism/existentialism, (f) Hegelianism, (g) naturalism, (h) Marxism, and (i) post-humanism, as well as finally, (j) some kind of quasi-solipsism (this random order is not accidental insofar as it does away with a chronological approach). These should be treated as available perspectives which can always make an appearance in this text to establish the diversity of points of view proper for this problematic. For various reasons, each of the cases listed above—perhaps with the exception of the last, although even this is not fully certain—operates in a category of universal pretense which aims to exclude no one. And yet, how universal is the very challenge to know thyself? Is the self-reflexivity contained in this slogan, the peculiar relation between x and x, the auto, anything universal, or is it perhaps local? Is it ultimate or merely an episode? Is it inevitable, a feature of the species, or perhaps no more than a discursive event, a fleeting product of speech or cultural conditioning? Is it common or exceptional, popular or posh, historically constant and recurrent, or unique and without precedent?

Whoever is to answer the question of self-knowledge must roughly know who they are, or at least assume that he knows it, or assume that he can know it: he must also have the experience of knowing or attempting to know himself, or perhaps a sense that he has such an experience. This experience or sense is the only thing he can count on other than other texts on the topic (that is all concerning the methodology of this essay). He risks that he will engage with something fictional, perhaps something that only exists insofar as one thinks or speaks about it: something which assumes reality only in the act of thought about what and whether it is. Can something that exists in this way be a serious object of knowledge?

There is another risk related to the extent to which the categories listed above, despite their pretense to and desire for universality, are inevitably exclusive. They are all, of course, concepts of philosophical good faith and goodwill—the kind of good intentions that pave the road to hell. What should be done with all of those who for whatever reason are excluded or circumvented by this ancient call to know thyself? Those who cannot take up the challenge due to objective conditions? One cannot doubt or forget even for a moment that they constitute the overwhelming majority of people even though nothing seems more human and universally accessible at first glance, at least in its intention, than this noble call which from the very beginning suggests itself as the most important of the ten calls engraved on the stele at the entrance to the temple (incidentally, there have been two most important universal propositions in the Western tradition: the Greek "know thyself" and the Christian "love above all"; post-Christian modernity added one more: "break the shackles"). And yet we are perfectly aware that this ancient call is also the call of authority, it is not politically neutral but fits well within the existing hierarchies partly by referring to privilege and partly by legitimizing its exclusivity, and partly also by transforming this privilege into an instrument of control and guidance by which the function of self-rule is generalized into the regime of universal rule—how many complications, dangers and ideological trappings! Perhaps by excluding, segregating and stratifying, encouraging to contemplate, and at the same time by reserving a claim for the establishment of the paramount and highest task for "every man" it dissuades from tasks which are in fact more urgent, practical rather than theoretical, and morally pressing?

On yet another hand, one of the senses of the challenge to know thyself, which can definitely be considered compromised nowadays, at least no longer defensible in the context of world history, is the belief that self-knowledge leads to self-rule in the strong and global sense, that self-knowledge gives real sovereign independence, self-governance—not merely a substitute in the form of an otherwise attractive subjugation of others but real power in the sense of the capacity to realize one's best conceived good. The silent assumption here is the old fashioned philosophical belief that man, both as an individual and as humanity in general, can reasonably guide himself.

10

However, the experience of the 20th century (not only this one, but it shall suffice) teaches us, insofar as history can teach at all, that man as individual and as humanity in principle does not follow reason, or rarely does at best. He at most uses it occasionally, in a limited way and for limited purposes, but not as a decisive rule, and the hope that he could follow reason is the mother of the naïve, although at the dawn of the Enlightenment it was the mother of the very promising: progress, emancipation, secularization and other *enfants prodigieux* all of whom, however, went astray and rebelled against the kindly Enlightenment. In this sense, one can authoritatively assume that the challenge to know thyself neither fulfilled its promise nor did it, or so it would appear, go to the very core of universal human interest and care. As such, it is at least partly a deception or, to put it more delicately and to give it more justice, a tribute usually paid to beautiful ideas by disillusionment—it is an illusion, a self-deception, a fiction beautiful and sublime, only by which does man become an interesting animal, to borrow an expression from Nietzsche.

Let us note that cultures other than the West tend to avoid granting the challenge of self-knowledge such a high priority: the principle often manifest in the non-Eurocentric consciousness and once referred to, in the perhaps overly essentializing manner, as "Eastern" grants ultimate importance to "the unification with being in general" rather than self-knowledge. According to this conception, proper knowledge abolishes the very self by cancelling out the individuality and subjectivity of being and by dissolving the mind in All. The problem and program of self-knowledge is thus perhaps an episode which for some time, not too long, appeared in one local culture and civilization undoubtedly based on a very lavish, costly and energy consuming concept of individual happiness understood as prosperity and the right to secure welfare, beyond the law of natural selection, and to an all-inclusive life where everyone can be satisfied with being who they are.

However, the relative massification of consumerist wellbeing seems to be a historically transient phenomenon. There are already signs of a clear retreat from the conception of the universal attainment of the prosperity state where human individualism and its elitist, although now much more available, program of self-contemplation and self-knowledge develops the best. Certainly, Westernization has made this project the property of the entire planet. However, whether it will prevail or not is no longer being

11

determined exclusively within the bounds of Western civilization. There is and will continue to be a growing importance of a specific far-eastern Chinese and Confucian reformation which, due to austerity measures imposed by the conditions of late capitalism and a dynamic inflation of raw materials prices, will probably exert a strong pressure tightening the space available to an individual and his material freedom which is currently based on lavish individual consumption and cost-ineffectiveness. It is true that the Chinese turbo-capitalist boom of the last quarter century has generated new specific models of narcissistic egocentrism in China (the famous already proverbial new Chinese middle class and the one-child generation)[1], introducing into the Chinese domain of collectivity an element of an ambiguous and complex impact which may bring about an East-West fusion in the long run. However, even this compromise whose toxicity is difficult to predict already seems to marginalize the subject of our considerations making it an idea which is rather passé and does not bring any energy or hope into the future, an idea which no longer heralds anything.

Due to these transfers in the geopolitical centers of management which take relative significance away from the Atlantic and displace it to the Pacific circle[2], the principle of the "dissolution of the self" may gain political gravity since it will determine the paradigm at the center of the management of the masses, masses whose number will surpass anything we witnessed in the 20th century, with 13 billion earthlings predicted in the next century. Much suggests that Know Thyself may be a passing slogan, slowly and quietly fading into the past, if not a smoke screen for a post-expansionist civilization at the dusk of its dominance and the end of its historical significance. Perhaps by engaging with its essentialist intellectual priorities we merely exercise the noble art of meditation on lofty ideas of the past and our own forever lost past glory (although for a Pole, such as myself, this "ownness" is something

---

1 M. Jacques, *When China Rules the World*, Penguin Books 2012.
2 The Atlantic principle, by reference to Atlantis, puts forward before the civilization of this region the quest for lost perfection, wholeness and paradise. Atlantis, as one of a kind, suggests the singularity and individuality of what is perfect. The Pacific principle, on the contrary, leads civilization away from a one and only perfection toward pacification, balance, harmony and adjustment—this is the paradigm of perfection there, not a full and awesome singularity, but order and harmony for the whole: *yin-yang*.

additionally unobvious, by correspondence and on parole). Let us think of how provincial and, *pardon le mot*, parochial we are in this activity—here, somewhere at the peripheries of the former empire of European civilization, one which is currently steeped in crisis and destined to never again, at least in the foreseeable future, play first fiddle in the international orchestra, someone is sufficiently concerned with antiquarian noble ideas that they engage with something so long gone, outmoded and devoid of any power to mobilize and directly describe actuality as Know Thyself.

2. The Subject between Extremes

It seems that everyone who has any experience with knowing himself knows that it is an unlimited, unclear and rather hopeless endeavor. As to the ontological definitiveness of its object, the knower oscillates between a sense of immediate access to it, "himself as such" (after all, who knows better who I am than I do?), and its mediation by specific and not easily graspable or definable concepts, structures and narratives which constitute the discourse of self-reflexivity; between the intuitive substantiality or presence of "selfhood" and its empirical transience and elusiveness, its non-obviousness. Descartes relied overly on the first and made it into an independent substance; the final consequence of the latter was drawn by Hume who negated the reality of the "I".

By the same token, the more concrete expressions which I can ascribe to my "I" sometimes take a somewhat definite form and sometimes dissolve into indistinctness and hesitation. I am a given *this*, I possess *such and such* properties: I am this body, a human being, a Pole and a white middle class heterosexual man. I am also a mind, a desire, a combination of feelings and a certain malleable character. It happens that I think. Sometimes I think about myself. Sometimes I think in a focused and problem oriented way. And sometimes I think in the opposite way, dispersed and carefree, associationally. I often experience tiredness and my thoughts lose their contours, they flow one into the next in an uncontrollable and confusing way. Sometimes I think that the answer to the question of who I am is simple and unequivocal, and sometimes that it is limitlessly complex and unclear. The object which I am seems have a wave-particle dualistic nature, it is ungraspable and uncertain, incomprehensible and indirect, and infinitely mediated—yet this dialectic does not lead to any synthesis. Abandon all hope, ye who enter here, everything flows, everything dissolves. We are bound by this circularity (in one of its countless variants) familiar as an old joke: I, as in, "who?" as in, a soul. But a soul is also a mind. And what is the mind? Is it reason? And what is reason? Is it a thinking thing? And what is that? It is I. I am I—an old truth, empty and boring, as is best shown in Fichte.

These oscillations and circulations can be directly responsible for a psychological imbalance threatening those who give much time and effort to self-contemplation. Such introverts, or rather introspectors, usually make the impression of being unnerving, unpredictable and capricious, somewhat detached from reality, and dedicated to matters which are not necessarily safe or reasonable (although here one often adds, with certain pity, that this applies only to the individual in question). Excessive self-knowledge, which often amounts to an extremely broad and detailed, if not petty, awareness of this lack of clarity, the knowledge of one's own ignorance with all its question marks, all possible self-interpretations, is in principle suspect and difficult to distinguish from egocentrism and narcissism. Who does not know this impatient and slightly humiliating feeling one gets when someone across the table *overly focuses on himself* instead of focusing *on us*. The explosiveness of this matter can only be heightened when that someone makes it into a constant and frequent practice which upholds its own claim to privileged status and sets its own conditions. It may lead to asocial beliefs and behaviors and away from what is beneficial, profitable and justified; such a person can also be non-solidarizing, insensitive and devoid of empathy. Political critics may accuse self-contemplation of being detached from the more urgent and paramount social problems and the adherents of raw mercantilism may take issue with how complicated it is to commercialize it—although ultimately no thing can not be commodified, self-contemplation commodifies reluctantly and requires that its marketers employ sophisticated and cost consuming mediations. Despite the facts that self-contemplation is a form of knowledge and that knowledge seems to be rational by definition, self-contemplation dangerously borders on the territory of irrationality, sometimes leading to madness which, of course, does not have to compromise it ultimately. It oscillates between being on one's own—"In thinking I am free, because I am not in an other, but remain simply and solely in touch with myself"[3]—and the second extreme of the pendulum, an escape from all one's content, as in Artaud when he says "My thought abandons me at all stages"[4]: between

3   G. W. F. Hegel, *The Phenomenology of Mind*, trans. J. B. Baillie, Humanities Press 1977, p. 243.
4   A. Artaud, *Correspondence with Jacques Rivière*, in: *Antonin Artaud: Anthology*, City Lights Books 1965, p. 7.

the totality of substantialization and a total de-substantialization, between fullness and emptiness, being and nothingness.

The intellectual history of modernity can be divided into two periods. The first is the egocentric and the second is the post-egocentric: the Cartesian kingdom of the subject and the Freudian republic of the subject dethroned and decapitated, that is, the harsh rule of the substantial self and its subsequent fall to the rule of the fragmented subject, "conflictual" rather than harmonious, weak and devoid of sovereignty. And is this not reflected in political history in the transition from citizen to mass society? The subjective oscillations placed at the pivot of the egocentric order may be the source of the undulating waves of modernity, the one and only epoch wherein man is understood as the causative self. This is precisely the egocentric epoch whose essential and apparently solved question is whether the human subject, man as self, is sufficiently causative and free, sufficiently autonomous to steer its own history to progress, to something better; or perhaps, regardless of all its talents, predominantly in science and technology, all its impressive inventions, humanity ultimately does not constitute itself as universal rationality but goes in the direction where the development of science and technology will merely heighten its capacity for universal suicide, self-destruction, with no chance for self-salvation. The recent history of technology is ultimately also the history of subsequent scenarios of the technological end of humanity: from the nuclear bomb, to the robot rebellion, to the now clearest post-atomic scenario of natural disaster due to the catastrophic ecological costs of universal human civilizational and material development (according to some estimates, even now we consume more resources than can be replenished by the planet's ecosystem). All this seems to point to the fact that humanity is facing some form of ecological catastrophe, the question being whether it will be local or global, with the inevitability of fate meted out precisely by the development of science and technology (it is also due to this development that the details of this possible ecological suicide are better known to us).

As we remember, Socrates advised Alcibiades to know himself in order to govern others.[5] From its very inception political philosophy promised that, or asked whether, indepth self-knowledge, an understanding of what one is, is

---

5   M. Foucault, *The Hermeneutics of the Subject: Lectures at the Collège de France 1981–1982*, Picador 2005, pp. 25–42.

the right step toward an adequate management of common affairs. Perhaps recent history, especially the present day which so emphatically shows us that human affairs do not move in reasonable directions and, despite local victories, rationalization as the grand narrative no longer has adherents even among those who can see no hope outside of it, provides the best evidence for how little the development of science and technology has to do with human self-knowledge. They will allow him to destroy himself more readily than to know. They also undoubtedly make the task of human self-knowledge all the more difficult by constantly changing him, transforming him, distancing him from "nature" and alienating him from what is "primal". At the same time, they expand him and create new senses of subjectivity in him, new functions, activities, domains of interest and self-development, new possibilities for action, production, creation and destruction. Does man not get to know himself by building pyramids, landing on the Moon or by organizing a holocaust as well? Does he not thereby explore the infinity of his potential and discover more and more about himself? The-Moon-Computer-Auschwitz-Hiroshima is a previously unknown horizon of humanity itself, opened before 20th century man by science and technology.

3. Genesis: The Socratic-Platonic Deception or The Irrepressible Need for Immortality

Perhaps it was all about an ordinary deception from the beginning. There's room for much abuse here. First of all, the self as such (*auto to auto*): does it exist at all? What is it? And what is it for? Second of all, there is the "knowledge". Assuming that there is something to be known at all, can it actually be known? Can there be an ultimate proper answer to the question of who I am? Or, are we being snared, trapped or led astray, into an area of subjectivism without criterion? "Know Thyself" began its career atop the gates of the temple of an oracle who issued prophesies in the form of riddling and ambiguous, if not straightforwardly nonsensical, utterances. Can one think of any worse credential than this? At the same time, it is obvious that the slogan itself rests on an ambiguity—it is meant to be a promise as much as an initial condition. It suggests that one will know one's deepest truth on one hand, and that one will not know it unless one knows himself first, on the other. Incidentally, it is usually cautiously assumed that it referred to the modus operandi of the Oracle itself rather than the general call for self-contemplation. Be that as it may, the titular principle already turns out to be unclear and rather sly at its source. What does it actually mean that we are encouraged to know ourselves by magic and its mumbled language of spells?

Socrates was ultimately a fraud as well, or at least someone who issued empty promises, since his "know thyself" ultimately led to what is known by the wisest, namely to the disappointing "I know that I know nothing". The additional element was the patronage and extra sponsorship from Pythia who made him "the wisest of men"[6] laying the foundations of one of the best public image campaigns in history which was carried out by Plato and has been successfully impacting audiences until the present. One has to remember that the background to this operation was a decline of the authority of the Oracle at Delhi as the centre of knowledge of the Greeks.

---

6   Plato, *Apology*, trans. G. M. A. Grube, in: *Plato: Complete Works*, Hackett Publishing Company 1997.

First Aeschylus and then Euripides ventured to critique the oracle in the context of what can arguably be referred to as ancient secularization. The Platonic reaction was meant to restore the sacred, although based on new principles which were partly initiated within Orphism. Plato undoubtedly used Pythia with no illusions, instrumentally, in order to propagate his own transcendent notion of "the navel of the world". The spiritual singularity of the daemon was thus discovered under reformed-religious, anti-hedonistic and radically anti-naturalistic auspices, in the name of which Plato established his spiritual/idealistic system, turning even Socrates into an idea.

And yet the "I know that I know nothing" as the only truth of the call to self-knowledge seems deep even today. No wonder! This is about as much as we know about ourselves. All we know is that not a lot is known, but then again, everyone knows this. So, let us be frank, Socrates did not invent anything especially awesome here. All he did was beguile his audience, till now, with a mirage of the sacred: the good which somehow *a priori* declasses everything else in that audience. This sacred and absolutely good is supposed to be discovered through a noble path, the noblest of all, the path of self-knowledge, in the context of an individual. This mirage of "an individual immortal soul" was given the splendor of the absolute and placed at the centre of the cosmos by Plato (by doing so Plato fundamentally reworked the Greek conception of the world and fit it into his peculiar cosmo-psycho centric paradigm: compare the isomorphism between the order of the soul and the order of the polis). That was the new "navel of the world"—the soul. However, the deceptiveness of the ideological revolution introduced by Socrates was uncovered and violently opposed by the Athenians early on, perhaps too violently, although this really was a matter of life and death, and so none of the parties could compromise. (Ancient Greeks, as is commonly known, did not imagine any positive individual immortality, any absolute goodness of the soul, and thus were not "good-souled"—not much good awaited an ordinary mortal after death and in order to deserve the Elysian Fields one had to perform rather extreme feats of heroism in the Greek opinion.) Socrates, for the sake of the cause and to avoid shame, chose to trudge ever deeper into that deception and to accept the sentence and go through martyrdom to give testimony to faith in the soul, which convinces many even today, than to give ground. However, as the story shows, the attempt to capture the self as an immortal soul and the "absolute good" was recognized by the audience as bearing the mark of something highly suspect and unreliable, excessive and exalted, from the beginning. It is possible that the Athenians were not any more naïve than we the contemporary people are and that the idea of defining what one is through what is divine and immortal, from out of this world, entirely independent from the *physis*, may not be too far from "corrupting the youth" and "blasphemy", quite against what Plato the PR master managed to sell to subsequent generations of Socratophiles.

Ultimately, having joined the sad parade of conservative number one hits in the crusade for the benefit of the plenipotentiaries of global capitalism, the conception of an immortal soul ends up being an assistant to the executioner. It makes for the preferred argument in favour of harsh punishment and maximum punitiveness in reaction to the "bad will" or "bad choice"—the metaphysically understood "rational subjectivity" of the perpetrator. It is not a coincidence that the harsh spokespeople for police morality ever since the time of Kant learned to high-mindedly and humanely combine a belief in the fundamental rightness of capital punishment with a love of traditional metaphysical categories. They are consoled by an idea which appears to be the building block of an argument known so well to the inquisitors and precious to any executioner in general: whoever they may be, those who are immortal cannot really be murdered, they merely experience the inflicted death of the body. Torturers should have an extraordinary interest to believe in immortality. The rest of us sense, with more or less intuitive certainty, that whoever answers the question of who they are starting with the immortal and the divine in us simply writes cheques for very large sums which they cannot cover. Only the majority of the interested parties, despite the worst premonitions, choose not to admit them in front of others as well as themselves as if the intuition commonly shared by mortals that death ends everything once and for all were an embarrassing taboo, in the same league as dropping a fart. This intuition might stem from the merciless instinct known as self-preservation whose sole concern is undoubtedly the body and not some soul. This is precisely why, despite its formal correctness and mathematical-rational impeccability (scientificity?), Pascal's reasoning regarding the belief in immortality (strictly speaking in god, which amounts to the same in this context) the so-called "wager", has not convinced anyone yet who was not already convinced—this arguably includes Pascal himself.

Montaigne, both loved and hated by Pascal, already had a lively interest and was rather skeptical about whether believers hold their beliefs seriously—first and foremost, in immortality; and whether they really fear god. "If we had a single drop of faith, we should move mountains from their place, says the Holy Word [...]. Some make the world believe that they believe what they do not believe. Others, in greater number, make themselves believe it, being unable to penetrate what it means to believe." And almost all that people do, customs, daily life, moral standards etc. is relative, dependent on the circumstances; little suggests that people seriously take into account the perspective of immortality and divinity, at the individual level the belief in the soul and in god seems to be a "weak" phenomenon (it is a different matter when religion is instrumentalized). "See the horrible impudence with which we bandy divine reasons about, and how irreligiously we have both rejected them and taken them again, according as fortune has changed our place in these public storms."[7]. Pascal knew that very well too. Montaigne did not lose any sleep over this common, hidden and private, impiety of man and his natural skepticism regarding man's self-perception as immortal. Instead it made him into a moderate relativist, cheerfully and southerly ironic when it came to virtue but not virulent or bent on negating the "natural norms of decency". The more northern and less sunny Pascal, on the other hand, precisely due to the weakness of his faith—where weakness is something spiritual, inner and fundamental for the self-knowledge and self-understanding of man, usually compensated for by ritual, institutional, educational and cultural power (in which aspects religion has been losing its monopoly due to modern secularization)—fell into misanthropy and melancholy, grief and bitterness. This feverish and maniacal state, which worsened quickly and led Pascal to premature death, was caused by a lack of evidence in the power of faith from both external worldly experience and, *the horror*, the inner introspective experience. Faith and fear of god are hardly motivating and do not saturate anyone other than perhaps a few weirdoes: they do not constitute any hard core of the soul. Immortality and divinity are hardly present in human life, especially for what they are supposed to be—in fact, no one bothers over them and it is difficult

---

7   M. Montaigne, *Essays*, trans. D. M. Frame, Stanford University Press 1958, Book II, Chapter 12, p. 322–323.

to find anything which might prove, verify or suffice to authenticate faith. And the higher the spiritual requirements toward oneself and the world are raised, the harder it is to find that evidence: Pascal was one of those who literally tormented themselves over the fact that they cannot find proof for the existence of faith. It led him to the verge of religious insanity. If it is not the essence of man in general to tend to avoid betting too heavily on immortality and divinity but to treat it as something of a spiritual distraction and abstraction in which not to invest much, it is the truth of modern secularized man. Montaigne and afterwards Pascal captured it each in his own way, as the private problem of an individual, something in the face of which one needs to reconfigure the problem of selfhood.

In the Platonic-Socratic deception which seeks to convince us that the truth of individuality is the immortality of the soul and knowledge of the divine in the Platonic sense of what is unchangeable, model and perfect, this general fraud can also be divided into a series of more detailed "moments" of false individuality where the soul dissolves into what is general and becomes subservient to the political, moral or cosmo-rational regime. This stands to reason given the cultural notion of an individual as a dependent part of a greater whole and its related lack of the notion of "the internal world" understood as separate, private and self-sufficient. As we know, for Greeks, the question of privacy and "the private interior" was instead a matter of the architecture and economy of daily life: what was private was the home, the household. In this context the soul was something "public", operational only within a community and absent outside of it, as has been suggested by Hannah Arendt in *The Human Condition*, for example. Socrates violated this order although he did not go beyond it. His God was no longer a municipal god but, due to his individualization, a general one, inchoately universal. It is this conception of the soul, as an inner *agora*, which gives rise to the conception of individual freedom as constituted within the inner hierarchy of faculties (passion, emotion and reason) as "self-rule", rational self-management by means of a subordination of desire to the supra-individual law or virtue. This is the source of the conception of subjective self-emancipation and at the same time self-reflexivity and self-reflection which create the free autonomous individual as the culminating state of self-understanding and self-transparency, although it simultaneously requires self-alienation from one's own desires—desire is in fact construed as something external here. This is why in Kant, and later in Hegel, individual freedom and autonomy come to be identified with subordination to a general reasonable duty and law. And when "the moral law within" is compared to the "starry sky above" it will precisely be because the *within* is as transparent, clear, ordered and glowing with light as the *above*: I understand myself well, I see myself in the rational, "natural light" (*lumen naturale*). I also understand what is good for me and where my interests lie. I clearly distinguish what I am not: my entire animal and carnal nature, and my lust-instinctive material condition.

However, the autonomy of the subject in its culminating articulation is indistinguishable from heteronomy—this is illustrated by the thesis found in Hegel's *Lectures in the Philosophy of History*, that one cannot be a moral subject if one lives outside the state (which, as may be worth noting, is itself this kind of subject). Starting with the Platonic takeover, the slogan Know Thyself leads to a knowledge of what is non-individual and the dissolution of the concrete individual in abstraction, "the objective spirit", the ideal truth, at least when picked up by the idealist. This is why even an ingenious and idiosyncratic individual such as Socrates turns into an unbearably moralistic, excessively idealized, irritatingly wise and impeccably virtuous figure in the context of the Platonic image campaign. Even irony and acrimony do not defend Socrates against the charge of alienatingly heroic and excessively saintly perfection. Plato goes so far as to claim that Socrates was never hungover or drunk, although he did drink, and that he could stand barefoot in the snow for hours—there are several other similar nonsensical remarks found in Plato. In this, Socrates as a concrete individual, with his weaknesses, ruptures and silly idiosyncrasies is utterly lost. The heroic figure of the philosopher forever encases his mundane individuality, which is untranslatable into any holy truth, into the marble sculptured muscles of the Platonic phantasm—it mummifies and canonizes it. And so we have knelt down in obeisance before the statue of Socrates for generations, although we well know that the truth of human self-knowledge cannot lie in such a sublime model. The whole thing smacks of some kind of deep dishonesty, phoniness and hypocrisy.

This is what various naturalists and materialists have always felt about the idealist, the believer, honest or otherwise, in immortal individuality. In various ways they followed the intuition that the promise of personal immortality is a swindle, perhaps sometimes underlain by good faith, which nonetheless does not change the crux of the matter: that in our existential economy immortality is the equivalent of "god bless you" in the economy of daily life, a security which is not backed by anything of value, and that this life is the only sphere in which to seek sense and value. The proper anthropological consequences of the finitude of human life, life as the one and only now (and not immortal eternity), develop in the materialistic notions of animality, biology, need, adjustment and civilization. The emancipation from the illusion of immortality also leads to the restitution of the absolute value of the body as that which is significantly individual, not simply the most *own* but identical with the self. Science plays an important role in this emancipation. However, naturalism ultimately dissolves individuality too since it robs it of its qualitative uniqueness and identifies all genius with "conditioning", genetic or environmental. It does not dissolve individuality in what is divine and free, but instead in what is determined: the generality and abstraction of the libidinal instinct, unconscious mechanisms, the environment, society and economics. It seems that here individuality is lost in what robs it of freedom and autonomy, in that which is "mundane", material and low-quality, devoid of any "higher sense" and/or goal. Here, freedom consists in doing without obstruction what we are forced to do by natural need/necessity (what we are determined to desire). One is tempted to "involuntarily" shrug one's shoulders over such a freedom. At first glance, the mechanism of desire is totally banal, forced and boring—there is nothing more automatic and repetitive than desire—and so if that is the ultimate sense and energy of individuality, then individuality must dissolve into the abstract blandness of something all too simple, petty and myopic.

Only psychoanalysis manages to convince us that the sense of desire as it stands is infinitely deep and fascinating. Psychoanalysis, as something of a modern theology of individual desire, shows how our desire bonds and shackles us to the Gordian knot of inner complications, histories, investments, sublimations and fixations—how our substantial depth turns out to be an amorphic "Lamella" (Lacan's term), yet at the same time the determinism of psychoanalysis is articulated through an extraordinarily poetic and dramatically powerful narration which imbues desire with what only theology can truly imbue, namely sublimity. Owing to psychoanalysis, our desires, even the silly ones, acquire a mysterious aura of something very deep, loaded with truths about us, truths of great importance, the sharpest of insights, something filled with meaning, imagination, symbolism and reference. Psychoanalysis is the theology and mythology of sexuality.

The same intellectual process which turns man into a material entity opens up the space of objectivity, and thus of science proper, and of technical relevance. Yet the failure of both the idealistic theological anthropology and the naturalistic anthropology of human life in the task of finally answering the question "What should man know as himself?" seems to lead inevitably to the final and most appropriate area of individuality, to that which is most concrete, unique, singular and idiosyncratic: the area of literature, and more broadly, of the written word. Literature, as well as its related forms of philosophical discourse, constitutes the domain of self-knowledge.

Ultimately, an individual man is neither reducibly a god nor an animal, machine or representative of a species—he is all of and at the same time something outside of this, he is something more, and it is that *something more* which constitutes the proper content and ultimate sense of the "self", an individual difference. The element of narration, with all its variants (myth, drama and above all prose), and all its characteristics, including what is usually referred to as "individual style", has always enabled the individual to articulate his most private and unique meaning—this is unprecedented and enduringly inscribed in the foreverness of things. And technology has always paid the element of narration momentous service. Film, theatre, the book, the internet and social media are all part of an ongoing development, a technical framework for the changing area of narration and self-narration (the telling-of-one's-self),[8] with all its psychological and sociological functionality: narration is the art by which individuals are constituted. These changing technical frames allow for an ongoing fluctuation of not only the object of self-knowledge but also of technology itself as well as the conditions of self-knowledge and the self-shaping of this object whose important trait is, after all, that his self-knowledge is, to an extent, his self-creation: the art of being oneself. Here, discovery partly overlaps with imagination and fantasy. The truth of the individual shines through in biographies, tales,

---

8   A. Macintyre, *After Virtue: A Study in Moral Theory*, University of Notre Dame Press 2007 (Third Edition).

episodes, anecdotes and the figures of life-stories. Outside of the general natural and social determinants which inform *this identity* I differ from others precisely through my own unique sum-sequence of sensations, experiences and events. This is the prose and poetry of an individual life. It somehow continually tells itself, weaving a sequence of signs, motifs, themes and stories as in a dream.

4. Modern Man: The Adventures of Robinson Crusoe

As is well known, Know Thyself is a foundational and source slogan. It constitutes Western man, as he was born in the Greek world: reflectively focused on himself as such, the singular-man, the individual subject, separate and ultimately lonely. Someone who thinks about himself, knows himself. And yet, as we have shown, the Greeks did not understand individuality the way it was understood in modernity or by "we" the 21st century people, with all the qualifiers and doubts. They did not understand it as a separate truth; for Plato its truth was an idea and in the more vernacular sense it was that which is common and which constitutes the political unity of all citizens. Certainly, as Hegel demonstrates in his *History of Philosophy*: "With this the infinite subjectivity, the freedom of self-consciousness in Socrates breaks out. This freedom which is contained therein, the fact that consciousness is clearly present in all that it thinks, and must necessarily be at home with itself, although eternal and in and for itself, must as truly be produced through me; but this my part in it is only the formal activity. Thus Socrates' principle is that man has to find from himself both the end and of his actions and the end of the world, and must attain to truth through himself."[9] Socrates was thus the first individual subject, the first "I think", and it was he who committed the source act of self-emancipation and returned to the self, although in this return he only discovered the divine and not himself. He only discovered thought, but thought that was turned against reality, against the body, by which he prepared the ground for Platonic and Christian metaphysics. This is why he made such an overwhelming career in the Christian world, that Christian *avant la lettre*.

The difference between modernity and antiquity when it comes to the general form of subjectivity and individuality is that modernity assumes the individual in itself as something internally infinite, boundlessly plastic, devoid of form and dynamic, as oppose to the static and limited ancient

---

9 G. W. F. Hegel, *Lectures on the History of Philosophy*, trans. E. S. Haldane and F. H. Simson, Humanities Press 1974, p. 386.

individuality inscribed into the form of the cosmo-political order. Of course, this is simplifying in the extreme; however, such an oversimplification can show us much of our own nature and so it should not be shrugged off as too grand a narration. Generally speaking, as is well known, the Greeks did not consider infinity to be anything positive. Everything has its limit, form, destiny, natural function etc. The world is a well ordered and closed cyclical-concentric place (whose center was Delphi). From the very center of the world issues the slogan Know Thyself which means, roughly, no more than *know the measure*, know what is within your limits, do not demand too much, and so on. Man is limited. He is an object of his own destiny and a "have-not of fate". Here, Know Thyself does not yet bear the mark of a heroically creative and shakingly limitless task; it was more like an instruction of the sort, Do your morning exercise!.

Let us get back to Plato for a moment. He did not go beyond these particular frames too much in his anthropology—although immortal and thus in a sense infinite, the soul is nonetheless part of the cycle of reincarnation and therefore does not leave the standard Greek closed circuit. With his typical contempt for the distinction between description and prescription, Plato also talks about the interior of the soul as a harmonious combination. First, it is a combination of general exo-simplicity with endo-complexity—from the outside the soul is something indivisible (and thus indestructible); on the other hand, so to speak from the inside, it is something complex and tripartite: it consists of the appetitive, willful and reasonable. This combination of simplicity and complexity is the first floor, perhaps the foundation, of the harmony which constitutes the soul. At the same time, we also have a vision of a second harmony, the hierarchy of these three parts, which constitutes the order and perfection of the "just soul", as opposed to the disharmony and dishierarchy of the soul of "the lowliest slave" where appetite governs together with emotion, harnessing reason for their own purposes. It thus turns out that Plato too ultimately stumbled upon a monster in the depths of the soul who explodes its form from within. Perhaps this makes him exceptional among the Greeks who tended to see evil as a quirk of fate rather than a result of sinful passions hidden inside man (as is explained by Nietzsche).

It is a monster in human skin. A multi-coloured and many headed animal: "Well, then, fashion a single kind of multicolored beast with a ring of many heads that it can grow and change at will—some from gentle, some from savage animals." Apart from that there is also, "one other kind, that of a lion, and another of a human being." These three—the monster, the lion and the man—are somehow mutually ingrown and coiled up in an individual so that "to someone who cannot see what is inside and only sees the outer shell, it appears as one living thing: man".[10] Few metaphors in the history of philosophy contain an equally awesome dimension of excess, explosiveness and breaching of all boundaries as this one, which is more reminiscent of the macabre visions of Bosch than the statues of Phidias. One is even tempted, perhaps with too much unctuousness, to ask Plato whether this monster, hidden in the interior of the human soul, possesses an "idea". Do passions and drives have ideal patterns in the world of essences? These questions, however undoubtedly petty, lead to another more serious one: Is it not that a perfect para-totalitarian state was necessary in order to subdue this monster? (Yes, all this to secure ourselves!) Is not the hidden truth of the conservative spirit of Platonism simply an excessive fear of the "tyranny of Eros"?

This is precisely the moment when an astonishing similarity between Plato and Freud, and the astonishing "relevance" of Plato and his most excessive intuitions, are discovered. And yet, modern man—who in his mature form is also the "Freudian" man—differs from the ancient man in that he was constituted in the dynamic movement of the loss of form (essence), that he broke up with "his measure" and became an infinity unto himself, that he absorbed infinity and ultimately turned "monstrous".

Ancient man was subject to his fate and destiny and modern man is the "lord of his fate" and the source of his destiny. Three grand "auto"-determinations lie at the root of modern man: autotelicity, autonomy and auto-constitution. Montaigne showed that individual man is an end for himself, his own object and the center around which the whole world revolves—the only point of view and the only source of sense and meaning of being. Shakespeare showed the new foundations of drama, the autonomous man who decides on his own and on his own account, which must lead to catastrophe: tragedy in its modern version. And finally, Descartes created the "I" as that which self-constitutes, and subsequent philosophers paved the road toward absolute freedom for this modern subject. It is this

---

10 Plato, *Republic: Book X*, in: *Plato: Complete Works*, p. 1227.

ideal of absolute freedom and the unlimited infinite power of subjectivity, as active (present in politics and civilization building) as it is self-contemplative (from Descartes and Bacon to the generations of Empiricists and Rationalists to Kant and Hegel, and even Husserl, Philosophy is one way or another identified with an inquiry into the mind/subject by the mind/subject itself), that guides modernity from its earliest period, through its classical stage, up to its mature form and its turn (Nietzsche and Freud). In the later modern or post-modern period, the collapse of this paradigm defines a landscape of decadence and perpetual crisis.

Thus, whereas the ancient Know Thyself is in fact a moralizing reminder of the existence of "boundary" and "measure" and the submission of man to a higher power or powers, the modern Know Thyself is more of an encouragement to explore the inner species-specific infinity and limitlessness of an individual man and humanity. You do not even know how much you are capable of. Hegel says, "The infinite peculiarity of particularity is what gives pretense and what is closely related to the subjective principle of the modern world."[11] And indeed, from Descartes, the subsequent philosophies of mind/the "I" discover in it subsequent variants of immanent infinity: from the theomorphic infinity fundamental for Descartes ("the innate idea of divine infinity"), to the anthropo-theological infinity of Hegel and the humanistic infinity of Feuerbach and Marx, to the biomorphic infinity of psychoanalysis.

The most controversial and mature confirmation of the existence of infinity within an individual found in modernity is the "discovery" of subconsciousness by psychoanalysis (and also, in his own way, by Nietzsche who was a near contemporary of Freud). Subconsciousness is in fact nothing more than another name for inner infinity, this time biomorphic and situated at the peculiar point between what is human and what is animal, within the hermeneutic bio-metaphysics of human instinct. This makes psychoanalysis the most atypical of inquiries—it is purely speculative and it possesses, to a large degree, a language of its own, a discourse on the unconscious impulsive substance of "my own self". One of the necessary

---

11 G. W. F. Hegel, *Elements of the Philosophy of Right*, trans. H. B. Nisbet, Cambridge University Press 1991, § 162.

consequences of this state of affairs in practice is that psychoanalysis, as the process of self-knowledge, never ends (Lacan).

For the ancients it was obvious that an individual is a unity. Even in the image of Plato's "absolute slave" cited above, the dishierarchy does not yet abolish the unity perceivable in the soul. Modernity, in contrast, constitutes an inner infinity as the opposite of unity, the radical disunity of the individual. It is comprised of an immeasurable series of events, vicissitudes, turns, sensations, experiences, conflicts, mistakes, lapses, breakdowns, traumas, symptoms, desires, possibilities, strivings and goals—the multiplicity of personality. General disorder and lack of any top-down frame or form: instead, multiplicity and variety of transformations, processes, embodiments and roles. Nietzsche's aphoristic explorations are perhaps the most drastic example of self-contemplation as an inquiry into one's own brokenness, dispersion and disharmony. The individual as multiplicity, heterogeneous. For Plato, who considered such a state to be the greatest evil (and the assurance that each man be one and one only to be the main task of the politics of justice), this multiplicity is the worst nightmare. Yet the individual is not one; he is a *multi*-vidual. An individual is not at all simple and indivisible, he is a *divide-ual*. Modern freedom and emancipation in general consist precisely in the freedom to be multidimensional, to go beyond a defined unity and boundary, to multiply incarnations on one's own accord and account, to actively play with identity.

Modernity understood, or rather brought about, that the individual is ruled by conflict and dissonance instead of harmony, order, hierarchy and reason; that he is not a state but a process; that instead of harmony there is oscillation between extremes; that instead of (moral) perfection one can at most dream of "fullness" (understood as the wealth of experience). And that ultimately the self is reigned over by disorder, mutability and the fluctuation of faculties, the final result of which is the triumph of irrationality and the collapse of reason, as has been brought to light by psychoanalysis. Of course, the ancients knew this problem as well. They recognized the inner conflict in man and understood the principle of "triumphant irrationality" (hubris). However, what went beyond proper measure in the Greek imagination was always met with "justice" which served as a standard and established boundary and norm. Modernity, in contrast, first deified human reason and made it lord of the world and then dethroned it, leaving it to the mercy of rebellious stupidity/madness. At the same time, man who counted on and was insured by reason fell into the captivity of the lowest instincts of the mass society in which people are no longer capable of self-knowledge because they have lost all subjectivity. This historical dynamic of modernity is also the inner dynamic of the individual himself—from reason to madness, from rule to downfall, from harmony to "psychopathy" and from progress to catastrophe. For this reason, modernity, and perhaps it alone, is the proper era of the singular man, forever separated from oneness lost.

This duality or polarity of modernity, which is reflected in the inner oscillation of man, can be illustrated with the help of two figures. On one hand, when modern man crowns himself lord of the world the peak image of self-reflection is the enlightenment vision of Robinson Crusoe, the protagonist of the first "novel" in the modern sense and one of the most popular books of the modern era.[12] Although he may seem trivialized by now, Crusoe's straightforward work of self-creation remains one of the major heroic episodes in the mythology of modern man—the hero of the bourgeoisie and of "white man". He is an early capitalist bourgeois figure of individual limitlessness, freedom and power, the fulfillment of all the desires impossible to realize by the ancient aspirants and technophants such as Sisyphus, Tantalus or Prometheus who were subjected to harsh repression by the Olympic regime for their attempts to take power and "technology" from the Gods (ambrosia, fire, etc.) In contrast to them, Crusoe—an ordinary English fellow, son of a merchant and at the time of going to sea no powerhouse but an everyman—in complete isolation on an island, owing to personal intelligence and tenacity, singlehandedly reconstructs, almost from scratch, human civilization (he only has several basic tools at his disposal). The inner source of Crusoe's unlimited power is benign and natural: it is ingenuity and survival instinct which give him strength, not some metaphysical depth. The outer resources, on the other hand, are knowledge and technology which Crusoe utilizes skillfully and with great praxiological sensitivity. Had he given himself to Socratic considerations he would not have survived. Instead, quite literally, he goes from being a castaway to not only an inhabitant of his island but

---

12 D. Defoe, *Robinson Crusoe* (1719).

also its ruler—he subdues its nature and turns it into his own productive enterprise. He also subdues the other, the "savage" Friday, who is saved from the cannibals and falls into the generous custody of the obviously higher and dominant Mr. Crusoe with equal ease as the rest of the island. Crusoe is "the king of the island" as he styles himself. Someone may remind us at this point that he also had a Bible, the only cult object which miraculously survived the shipwreck. However, it was not the source of his ingenuity, it was merely a psychological and sometimes medical prop. It was not the source of order on this decidedly ego-cratic and not theocratic island. Crusoe owes the rule of the island exclusively to his resourcefulness and strength and perhaps, above all, to his self-confidence, stability and tenacity—20 years of loneliness and fear of cannibals does not disrupt his psychological balance in the least. The source of Crusoe's success is that he knows who he is very well. However, his self-knowledge and self-understanding were not ungraspable [Crusoe had an engineering rather than a humanistic mind], and during his time on the island his identity did not undergo much change—27 years passes like a day and Crusoe does not even age too much, he is still the same person, astonishingly. As the son of a merchant Crusoe was not extraordinary, and he did not become anyone special or exceptional later on, despite his awesome adventures. He remained, as it is sometimes put, his old "self", a humble and hardworking self-made man.

Of course, here too there has to be some room for God. The adventures of Robinson Crusoe have a deep theological dimension, just like in Socrates, since they are both based on the conception of the privatization of the divine (this is a Socratic and not a Platonic motif; Plato was generally not friendly toward individualism and privacy, in which he went against his master). On his uninhabited island, Crusoe found God in nature and the happy twists of good luck which allowed him to survive, but most of all he found God in himself as if he had already always been there. Yes, he knows himself by knowing the God within. And it is a private God of Robinson Crusoe's own, to who he subsequently offers the bloodless sacrifice of a converted savage. The fact that Friday does not get slaughtered in the name of the Lord, not even in self-defence, is already a merit of enlightenment humanitarianism and evidence of Crusoe's rule over the island. Only cannibals are excluded. A close reading of fragments of The Phenomenology of the Spirit in which self-knowledge in the first act of its self-constitution devours what is alive only later to realize that it was another self-knowledge[13] suggests that Crusoe needed to murder the cannibals, above all, in order to erase his sense of guilt and mourning after the "first Friday", unnamed and nameless, who he devoured and whose bones are scattered about the island, although the event itself has been repressed—hence the slightly paranoid atmosphere of threat, proper to the horror genre, which prevails from the very beginning on the island constantly endangered by cannibals (in fact, of those "in us"). If the social relation is preceded, as Hegel suggests, by the relation of devouring, then the truth Crusoe did not know he knew is that he had to murder and consume the "first Friday" before he could save the next one and turn him into his subject. Is it the nagging sense of guilt which best explains Crusoe's career and success on the island? Or perhaps his conversion, his "return to God", was a form of penance.

It is undeniable that for Crusoe God was a fundamental source of support and the providential force of fate, whereas for Socrates, the source of judgment, caution and moral intuition. By communicating with God, Crusoe plugs into his energy and "charges his batteries", gains hope and comfort as well as company in a time of loneliness and siege from a cannibalistic imaginarium. He has a powerful friend in God, with who he carries out a dialogue—in response to Crusoe's postulates, there always appears some sign in the form of a citation from a randomly opened page of the Bible; opening books at random had generally been a well-known method for communicating with gods. Socrates' God is more intellectual, he is a discussant, critic, consultant and an alter ego. Everyone has what he or she needs, is the guiding principle of the privatization of God. The difference lies in the final effect. Socrates is a dramatic figure whose loyalty toward his God leads him to a tragic end, if not, in a sense, a divine one—his death has a dramatic setting and a spiritual dimension equal to the death of Jesus. Of course, it is not a defeat but a moral victory, a triumph of virtue which goes way beyond classic Greek tragedy. Crusoe, on the other hand, simply comes through his adventures alive. His success is prosaic but full: both moral and physical, and even business. Crusoe's success is thus not a battle victory but an achievement in enterprise—the triumph of human capability, potency

---

13 G. W. F. Hegel, *The Phenomenology of Mind*, pp. 220–227.

and steadfastness, an exercise of unlimited individual power available to every man. Here, the modern egalitarian message of Robinson Crusoe can be opposed to old-fashioned Socratic elitism.

There is one point that Socrates and Crusoe have in common: their clear common sense, unthreatened by any internal conflicts or mutually contradictory desires, their steadfastness in following the guiding force of reason. Both embody faith in the supremacy of rationality, which is either theoretical or practical but nevertheless always hegemonic and immune to instinct and passion. Neither Socrates nor Crusoe, as embodiments of reason, manifest anything which might indicate the work of the energy of libido and the economy of drives—there is no Eros or Thanatos in them. Even Socrates' suicide bears no mark of the self-destructive drive for death: it is instead a calculated spectacle of ethical intellectualism. Crusoe also never ponders the two phenomena one could not in fact avoid thinking about on an uninhabited island: sex and suicide. The powers of sexuality and (self) destruction remain, in both their cases, on the outside. Of course, in the case of Crusoe we can easily find them repressed and transformed through symbolic work (cannibalism, already mentioned, to which we may now add the crypto-homosexual bond with Friday) but their return is out of the question: Crusoe will not be haunted by any monster of the subconscious or nightmare fantasy borne of lust and violence. Crusoe is ideally free and crystal pure—a character profile which may have been significantly influenced by the puritanism of Daniel Defoe. His self-knowledge, apparently grounded in perfect self-transparency, is thus conditioned by repression and the deepest species of ignorance—one where we not only do not know but in which we do not know that we do not know.

In his first act on the stage of modern history, modern man appears as an optimistic and bright figure, a figure which is "destined to succeed" and who defines himself and the world through development and progress—the story of Robinson Crusoe is after all a tale of individual fulfillment, satisfaction, independence and self-subsistence, it is a "career" in the most bourgeois sense of the word.

What is the source of this incredible optimism of early modernity? Roughly between the beginning of the 17th and the end of the 18th century, for nearly two hundred years, man expected, entirely seriously and not without good reason, progress for and from himself, the independent creation of the good and the capacity to make a better reality—self-knowledge as self-governance and governance over fate. It is an era of reason, starting with Descartes' naïve maximalism and ending with Hegel's mature ("absolute") maximalism, the pinnacle and at the same time the last maximalism in the history of philosophy. It is an era of the belief in the ultimate rationality of man and everything in general: a pan-rationalism whose disturbance during the Restoration preceded by the loss of innocence during the Revolution will mark the beginning of mature modernity. Its crown anthropological figures—the post-Enlightenment figure of the determined man contingent on technocracy and the subject-generating mechanisms and techniques rather than the dictates of reason—will be built by Marx, Nietzsche and Freud (through psychoanalysis), and executed by mass totalitarianism. It is this schizoid "Nietzschean man" (a mixture of an *übermensch* and a premature pensioner: someone already old in their youth, or eternally young in their untimely senility), a dark and broken figure traversing the limbo of self-contemplation and self-searching toward madness, annihilation and mental darkness, hurtling between the maxima of desire and aspiration and the minima of humiliation, conditioning and autism. It is also, in its own way, an inhabitant of its own intellectual deserted island, one where there is no room for successful contest, only the ultimately suicidal plunge into a smoking volcano—it is this freak that opposes, or perhaps greets Crusoe with a bow, on the other bank of the river of modernity.

5. The Scientific Foundations of Modern Man

One may claim, with little controversy, that the appearance of early modern subjectivity was only possible due to the leap made in science and technology—they facilitated the arrival of the idea of plastic transgression and breaking the mold of form which dominates the imagination of Francis Bacon. According to a competitive thesis, forcefully propagated by Hegel, we owe this modern guiding principle of unlimited, free and self-standing subjectivity to Christianity. However, without questioning its significance, I think that other events turned out to be more significant. Those events took place at the beginning of the modern era when a series of breakthroughs in the scientific knowledge of the world not only changed the cosmological paradigm but also transformed the way man understood himself by providing an indubitable proof for the fact that science can significantly assist man in the task of self-understanding. This transformation involves a takeover of infinity: the construal of self-sufficiency and autonomy as proper to the man-creator as an entity no longer subject to any boundary or top-down measure (the first to stumble upon this idea was Pico Della Mirandola). In order to become himself in the sense of modern humanity, man had to take over God's power of creation (including self-creation). He had to become a creator, for which Christianity did not provide sufficient premises.

The Copernican turn was at first glance far from beneficial, it was even humiliating for man since it threw him off the cozy and distinguished place "at the center of creation" previously occupied by the Earth together with the progeny of Adam and Eve: the manager and administrator of things created and their static order. Inhabiting the center of the universe, man could even afford a tour of all its major metaphysical regions, as did Dante. The needs and functions of the center inhabited by man determined the functioning of the entirety of creation: the sun shines so that the center is bright and warm, the planets orbit in order to determine the vicissitudes of human life and history, the stars educate man on harmony and facilitate music, etc.

The pre-Copernican geocentric vision has its allure; it tempts with anthropocentric promotions and frequent sales of luxury goods—everyone is allotted his or her own star, everyone can find his or her own guaranteed spot in heaven for the reasonable price of obedience, and so on and so forth. In a compact, closed and wisely planned universe man appears to be relatively great and important, perhaps the most important, second only to God. And the foundations of the world appeared to be quite solid and durable—let us ignore the dark propaganda which sneeringly and falsely accuses this cosmography of the invention of such cantilevers as turtles, crocodiles and other beasts on which the world allegedly rests: people in those days could think sufficiently abstractly to do without them. This world is partly reminiscent of those miniature ships enclosed in glass jugs and bottles—it is surrounded by a kind of imaginary bubble of finitude beyond which there is only the transcendent infinity of God, only it and nothing else. This vision may be very calming as it suggests that reality ends right beyond the fence and does not extend into the infinite distance, which may indicate that somewhere out there lurks a repetition, another world just like this one (this vision was so hard to digest that, a mere four hundred years ago, Giordano Bruno paid the price of his own life at the stake for disturbing the public with this kind of folly). The world in a bubble suspended in an infinity and also understood as personal and caring, renders the pre-modern image of the world and the position of man therein very stable and well-balanced. No wonder it was not fast or easy to leave this bubble—man inhabited it with a sense of security and cosmic stability and in this sense the "middle ages" only appear to be an epoch of common anxiety to the most naïve. Therefore, the Copernican turn took much time to find its way into the collective human consciousness. Public opinion in principle always initially opposes the introduction of this kind of innovation.

The Copernican turn was one of the anthropological revolutions brought about by the development of scientific knowledge. After it, the decentered and banished man, as opposed to the earlier stable man seated at the center of the universe (which guaranteed man's pivotal position as the single spectator for who the show of nature is performed), begins to inhabit one of the many planets revolving around the Sun. He must unlearn the false pride of the one who is only second to God, the child of God, and grow up to be an adult, to stand on his own feet on the mobile and non-flat Earth, and to face the truth of the infinite universe in comparison to which his world is but a speck of dust. He must rid himself of the illusion of the cozy navel of the world where he had lived securely, napping by the fireplace at God's house. Instead he must understand that he inhabits a random sphere which together with other spheres drifts around yet another sphere, one of the multitude, perhaps an infinite series of such spheres, suspended in an infinite space. The sky does not cover him with a blanket; it is an abyss, a bottomless and brimless hole opening out to a limitless cold silence—"the eternal silence of these infinite spaces frightens me".[14] When compared to this infinity, man turns out to be infinitely small, insignificant, random, laughable and goalless, perhaps he is even a mistake. However, precisely because he is capable of anything, he is not limited, since this randomness is also freedom, variation, transformation and unfettered limitlessness. Man is lost in infinity but also finds himself in it, against the oversensitive and hysterical Pascal. He learns to use it, he recognizes it in his own natural universe, his milieu, he understands it as imminent, he transforms it like he does all other things into a "quantity" which is to say he "tames" it, scientifizes it, renders it calculable and predictable, and then he includes it in his calculus and equations of physics. This is how science changes his self-understanding and how naturalistic anthropology dethrones metaphysical theology once and for all. The Anthropocene and its theoretical foundations are laid; it is the epoch in the history of the Earth where the activity of man determines the situation of the entire planetary biosphere. Whatever enables the radical change in the self-knowledge and self-understanding of modern man also lays the foundations of technology. Such is the beginning of the era of the scientific-technological man.

Heliocentrism, the sphericity of earth and the infinity of the cosmos as fundamental turns in the early modern scientific knowledge of the universe must be supplemented by Newton's principles of dynamics: the first, that every object will remain in a uniform motion in a straight line, or at rest, unless compelled to change its state by the action of an external force, and the second, that when acted upon by an external force the object accelerates proportionally. These principles radically changed the face of ontology. Before Newton, physical being was understood as naturally static and immobile—matter was at rest. This led to the obvious question of what had first moved it and the hypothesis of the "first mover"—the first force

---

14 B. Pascal, *Pensées*, trans. W. F. Trotter, Dover Publications Incorporated 2003, § 296, p. 61.

which set physical being in motion and imbued passive matter with activity (animation, the action of the anime). As such, matter was rendered independent from what animates it. The Newtonian seemingly innocent "or at rest" was one of the "ors" which changed the course of history.

This "or" means that there is no difference between steady motion and motionlessness, and thus that being is mobile and may in principle last forever. It does not need a first cause since the universe is governed by dynamics and it is motionlessness that requires an explanation and a cause (motionlessness will ultimately be completely eliminated from physics; in the world of bodies nothing, absolutely nothing, stays at rest). Everything in the physical world is in motion and does not need any animation, does not need souls.

The naturalization of motion, the dynamization of being, has fundamental significance not only for the ontology of reality but also for the "ontology of the self", for the concept of an entity which is identified with the individual. The individual too makes itself dynamic and becomes by nature a motion, a process, something fluid rather than stable. Even the hard substantialism of the Cartesian "I" rests on something as fluid and fluctuating as thinking and thinking alone. However, post-Cartesian philosophers, both empiricists and rationalists, will quickly take up the task of the de-substantialization of the subject which will culminate in its *liquidation* by Hume (pun intended). At the same time, the autonomy of motion means, more generally, that the becoming of man is limitless, that motion cannot be exhausted and that given additional force it will accelerate. The energy and exertion of force no longer serves the sole purpose of conservation but leads to the acceleration, accumulation and aggregation of change. Here appears the idea of natural incrementation; the gain from the effort of existence is entirely different from what had previously been assumed—an effort leads to acceleration, it generates "value added" which goes beyond self-preservation. One may say that, at the fundamental level, being as such does not require a reason for which it "is" rather than "is not". It does not require the Leibnizian "sufficient reason": being from itself, it boils over from its own source, autopoietically, not by virtue of some separate initiative at odds with nothingness which would allegedly be "primal", as was assumed by traditional ontology where being follows from nothing (*ex nihilo*). In traditional ontology nothing is first and unto itself, and does not require a reason. Now, nothingness requires an explanation and a specific reason: if there were nothing it would be appropriate to ask why there is nothing rather than something. Here not emptiness but fullness is rendered obvious. Due to Newtonian dynamization, ontological nothingness is no longer an outer layer of being and a permanent threat which calls for continuous confirmation at the level of the "force of creation" (or re-creation), the "cause of existence". By the same token, being becomes energetically sovereign and autonomous when it comes to all alleged transcendence (the final identification in 20th century physics of matter and energy is a mere *ex post* costume for that dynamic modern ontology). And man as such also recognizes himself as "energy", as existent without the mediation of any external intervention, as a driving force capable of accelerating being through its own effort and industry, capable of accelerating becoming itself. Moreover, the fact that motion is self-acting, and motionlessness is only an exception within common mobility, marks the end of the world of established form and the birth of the world of change—everything changes, nothing lasts. "Being stuck in one place", against the world considered the prime example of perfection by Plato, is now compromising: he who does not develop, actually regresses. In a world where everything changes, man accelerates, he introduces dynamics into all dimensions of his life, which means that his "selfhood" also ceases to be an object and instead becomes a becoming, a life accelerated, intensified existence: energy. Owing to the growing speed of existence, human life becomes more and more saturated with content and events, and the experience of it is "massified"; being itself appears as a mass.

Since it embodies the principle of the dynamics of being, modernity necessarily turns all its main figures into their opposites—its dynamic generates dialectics as the principle of being and not merely the principle of understanding. This is why Crusonian individualism is also turned on its head by modernity and the early modern "optimistic" rational subject is confronted with the nihilistic irrational and "pessimistic" subject, conditioned by the mature and disillusioned modernity. It is confronted by Nietzschean man (who dreams of an *übermensch* and sullenly observes the contemporary condition) and its Zarathustrian doppelganger, the Freudian neurotic, as well as the doppelganger of those two, the Musilian "man without qualities". They all, each in his own way, embody the absolute dynamic of individuality, the combination of infinity and motion in its starkest form where naturalism is interwoven with metaphysics—in Nietzsche as the will to power and in Freud, as the death drive.

Before we elaborate on the problems sketched out above let us dwell a little longer on the history of scientific discoveries and how they changed the conception of the world and man as well as how the development of science influenced philosophical anthropology. There are several other cases we should note.

It may be sensible to begin with the rather unexpected remark that in the period only slightly preceding Newton's findings the early modern spirit of rational scientism, which saw the essence of precision and true knowledge in the then widely accepted mechanistic-mathematical program-paradigm that gave rise to extreme optimism and hope, was reactivated by Spinoza in his own science of self-knowledge and emancipation in the context of mechanical determinism (the early modern hope would generally be abandoned in the following century, although it would return over the next several hundred years in various forms and guises). Spinoza ingeniously applied knowledge *more geometrico* to self-knowledge whose principally emancipatory function lies in the knowledge of the fact that one is not free in the sense presupposed in the concept of the "free will" and the anthropomorphic-teleological vision of the world. It lies in the recognition that one is fully determined within the order of a reality which is fundamentally without alternatives—the task is merely to know the proper causes and mechanisms and to drop the illusion. What remains controversial is the extent to which Spinoza can be of use to anyone other than himself. Although, if his system was as useful to him as he suggested, and as is suggested by his biography too, it would be a sufficient intellectual legitimization of his project. Spinoza's vision of reality was perhaps the only attempt to do the hard science of oneself: reflexive hard science. Spinoza's individualism and its rationalistic context also indicate an interesting counterpoint for the rational individualism of Robinson Crusoe—the man of contemplation and the man of action have something in common after all: the assumption that the individual, in principle, is guided by his rationally recognized own good and that this recognition is within reach, even if "all things excellent are as difficult as they and rare".[15]

---

15 B. Spinoza, *Ethics*, in: *Spinoza: Complete Works*, trans. S. Shirley, Hackett Publishing Company 2002, Book V, Proposition 42, p. 382

6. The Evolution of Modern Man, Nietzsche's Moustache, The Fittest Man and the Man Without Qualities, The Four Pillars of Modern Man

Newtonian dynamism finds its paradoxical and contradictory supplement in the second principle of thermodynamics: the increase in entropy. It states, against the idea of the autonomy of motion, that every order is costly and that the cost of order is a more general increase in disorder, that an increase in complexity requires an effort on the part of chaos which itself also increases and that fatigue and exhaustion are the only ultimate "goal" of progress and motion. Mechanics is optimistic, while the later thermodynamics plays a darker tune which ultimately leads to ontological nihilism and a lack of hope. Certainly, the discussion regarding the potential "heat death of the universe" also involves the question of its expansion—the winner will either be the principle of motion (provided that the expansion marks the defeat of the growing entropy) or the principle of the exhaustion of motion, a universal frost. However, it is also true that scientific cosmology introduces time scales of unprecedented orders of magnitude into the image of the universe and it gives a perspective of extreme duration and slow becoming to cosmic and natural processes. By doing so, it distances the question of the ultimate destiny of the cosmos from the dimension of human life so much that general eschatology loses its rationale. And even if the most intellectually flamboyant conceptions of the world put forward in the classical modern era (by Hegel, Comte and Marx) were still after some rational culmination in the form of a teleological vision of an arrival point, the omega, mature modernity must clearly do without it, which of course does not preclude the appearance of cheaper substitutes.

The principle of entropy implies that being, apart from dynamic spontaneity, is also imbued with futility and that it is utterly "for nothing". The possibility that the destiny of existence is simply death and exhaustion, that even the universe must die, means, for man, that his life *sub specie aeternitatis* is just an idle effort and empty torture. The irreversibility also precludes the hope of repetition or return, the regularity of goodness and saturation—here, what is regular is exhaustion, anxiety, spasm and breach. There are no prospects for comfort and satisfaction and all good must be paid for with an increase in evil. There is no innocent being and however virtuous and kind you may be you facilitate an increase in the sum of all harm by virtue of mere existence. In philosophy, the response to this will be Schopenhauer's metaphysical pessimism—a combination of dynamic spontaneity and entropic futility in one principle: "Will".

Much has been said about the importance of the science of evolution for philosophical anthropology and the concept of man. Much like the Copernican turn, it also seems to be "one grand humiliation" where man turns out to be a product of nature instead of the image of God—for some lovers of tradition, even today, the concept of "kinship with the ape" amounts to an intellectual scandal. Yet, just as heliocentrism gave man a proper notion of his place in the cosmos, and with it, real power instead of childish fantasy, so too, evolution gives him pride by showing that he is the most advanced and promising product of nature: capable of virtually unlimited advancement, advancing "by nature", an expansive and conquering "man of success". In this context, evolution introduces into philosophical debate the liveliest conflict and the greatest problems, including political ones, which modern humanity has ever had to face.

The first question is of the right interpretation of Darwinism itself: what does "survival of the fittest" actually mean? Who is the "fittest"? Who will survive and what does it mean to survive? What will survive in the end? Prior to evolution, these issues had been within the purview of speculative theology formulated in terms of salvation as well as its sense, criteria and conditions; now they have been secularized and turned into questions of the sense, criteria and conditions of "survival" or "life success". As such, these questions open up the entire naturalistic and moral problematic related to egoism and altruism. From the very inception of modernity (see Hobbes and Spinoza) until today (Game Theory and the Prisoner's Dilemma), the question of what is one's own good and how individual interest should properly be understood remains a primary problem in the context of human self-knowledge. How should I play in order to win? Should I cooperate or not? Should I help the weak or let them perish? And the most fundamental question: what does it mean to win and what are the criteria for victory? Who wins? How and why? What is and what should it all be about?

The category of game, which is significantly the game of winners and losers and thus is no mere playtime but something dead serious, best encapsulates the modern change in the existential dynamic of an individual. Here, the elements of rivalry, fight and race enter life—the fight for survival is the second classic cliché of evolution. The principle "do your works and receive thy prize" is transformed into the new one, "do what you can and maybe you will succeed". At the same time, the pluralism of the modern world is only as broad as the number of variants and versions of victories and victorious strategies it allows. As with every paradigmatic principle, evolution seems to introduce certain limitations and reduce multiplicity to uniformity: the majority must lose, *point de reveries!*

The core of the issue is that evolution reduces all criteria to materialistic ones. It is not that the question of victory boils down exclusively to the number of offspring produced—culture and its own extra-biological stakes also enter the game. However, there is a common denominator here: evolution changes the perception of hierarchy insofar as it focuses vision and judgment on the question of individual adaption and the effort to secure and expand one's own being. Everyone must evolve on one's own: work, act, produce, accumulate resources and "do one's best". This is another consequence of evolution, although it again remains unclear what it all means other than that, however one may understand one's defeat and source of frustration, its main cause is always and above all one's own "maladaptation". On the other hand, as was well known already to Hobbes, there is no absolute success or ultimate victory—each life remains unsaturated and each satisfaction is merely a temporary break after the fight and a preparation for another round. Only death brings rest—how far have we gone from the Greek conviction of the attainability of satisfaction such as the Epicurean one! The difference may lie in the fact that Greek self-knowledge was aimed at moderation and consisted in the conscious management and judgement regarding one's needs which, understood properly owing to meticulous self-consciousness, turn out to be modest and easy to satisfy, not only in Epicureanism. Precisely this easiness forms the premise of the "Epicurean sloth" in the rhythm of friendly chats in the garden, healthy body and peace of mind. In contrast, the modern limitlessness of man, the fact that man is not the measure of all things but an immeasurable expansion and evolution of it, renders his desire endless and impossible to satiate: no one is ever satisfied with what he already has but wants more and more of what he loves best. This is the new source of human tragedy: let us call it Faustian, after Spengler.

Whereas the mechanistic thinking of early modernity introduced into being the dynamic of the principle of spontaneity and the acceleration of motion, the evolution of mature modernity appears to imply an additional principle of maximum possible acceleration and the infinity of growth: in the world of pervasive acceleration, only the highest and greatest instance of it can bring about victory in the game. Being becomes a race and the individual its participant—egalitarianism does not mean the abolition of hierarchy in the world, it merely means a certain dynamization (always limited and regulated by extra-meritocratic factors), an opening of a stiff structure onto inner motions whose dispersion and kinetics would not have been allowed by previous epochs.

For a single man and his self-knowledge this means that Know Thyself becomes a more or less fundamental element of the general "survival strategy", an element in the game of life, subservient to life and subjugated to its goals: disinterestedness recedes into the background and self-knowledge becomes functional (or dysfunctional)—it serves something more than itself. This is also how one of the most lucrative and still dynamically developing markets of modern consumption opens up: the consumption of self-knowledge, the commercialization of techniques aimed at its deepening and development, the psychological and psychotherapeutic industry, the popular sciences of the mind and cognition with all their weaknesses and strengths, the search for one's own path etc. This leads to the production of a huge domain of scientific as well as pseudo, popular and para scientific knowledge supplemented by disciplines of more ancient provenance but still alive in common social practice today: astrology, horoscopes, numerology etc. However, one should not hold these forms of self-reflection in contempt, they too are evidence that self-knowledge is not a pure abstraction.

Modern man must know, first and foremost, his weaknesses and strengths, whereas ancient man had to know his virtues and vices—this is another result of the evolutionary notion of life wherein individual existence becomes *fitness*. What does it mean to be strong? What does it mean to be the *fittest*? How does one gain power and what is power? This question is entertained already by Hobbes and if we associate it mainly with Nietzsche it is because this very question, the question of the maximum of life and the peak of power (what is true *fitness*?),[16] was his biggest preoccupation. It was the most urgent and most tormenting riddle of existence for this autistic recluse of shy disposition, sensitive and sickly, deeply afflicted by many physical and spiritual ailments, yet a maximalist who was euphorically in love with life as an open and infinite place in the "colossal power"[17]. Nietzsche combined the greatest weaknesses, the weakness of the body and mental imbalance, with the greatest spiritual tension and intellectual power, with clarity of insight and violent penetration. Was it a narcissistic dream of a weakling and "loser", who Nietzsche was according to all possible notions of modern bourgeois decency, which inspires similar spiritual wimps and pitiful ultra-ambitious intellectual neurotics until today? A dream, *a contrario*, of cruelty, absolute domination, irresistible authority, total intensity of being and radical self-affirmation? Or was it the first cry, too pathetic in its optimism to be taken at face value, of an individual submerged in the poverty and despair of being as a serious struggle and a real game of the will to power and thus as pressure, constant tension and the perpetual need to exert all of one's strength?

It is obvious, it must be noted, that the objective of the author of *Zarathustra* was to imbue the evolutionary self-knowledge of man conceived as a dynamic and unlimited potential for development—the knowledge which can be variously interpreted and understood—with fundamental and revolutionary as well as idealistic and maximalistic function and sense. This was a spiritually post-romantic dream of the highest reaches of human genius meant to bring about a comprehensive anthropological revolution, the transformation of all values, the end of Christianity and the dawn of a truly new era, the rule of the will to power—and all in the early modernist art nouveau style. One should perhaps attribute it to the "spirit of the epoch" that in his search for the possibility conditions and "best climate" for this enterprise Nietzsche, professor emeritus and one of the first beneficiaries of "social welfare", wandered into the wilderness of phantasmagoric aristocratism and brutal philosophical fantasy inhabited by humanoid and parody-of-man

---

16 Peter Sloterdijk's term in: You must change your life, trans. W. Hoban, Polity Press 2013
17 R. Safranski, *Nietzsche: A Philosophical Biography*, trans. S. Frisch, Granta Books 2002, p. 19.

creatures and beasts *à la* Conan the Barbarian. Perhaps already then, in the high era of steel and steam, although long before the epoch of the atom and the processor, the vision of such an amazing rise—the project of revolution in human values and the transformation of man, additionally conditioned by the "transvaluation of all values" (according to its self-proclaimed prophet) and put forward in the form of iterated metaphors—was built on utter naiveté. And perhaps already then it sinned with slight intellectual aberration and a psychological mania typical of reclusion, a certain infancy and a conspicuous fascination with cruelty. All in all, Nietzsche's naïve and ostentatious fascinations, somewhat justified by the spirit of the industrial era, sometimes bear the mark of a kind of intellectual "self-violation"—out of politeness one should perhaps not ask the question of what it actually means when a retired philology professor of mediocre height and posture entertains, with exaltation, the image of the "splendid blonde beast". Nietzsche appears to have fallen prey to the life ideal of infinite expansion as an interpretation of evolution. Yet perhaps he simply tried to raise the spiritual content of this ideal onto the highest "icy" planes which were at the same time the most idiosyncratic and "his", determined by his own obsessions, helplessness, bitterness and depression. This is precisely what makes him so extraordinarily interesting.

To paraphrase the Marx Brothers: this man may look insane, but let us not be fooled by appearances—he really *is* insane. Question: if I am so powerful, then why am I so weak, and so, who am I ultimately: a lion or an ass? Or maybe something even worse, like the last man, the last representative of "a teeming mass of worms"[18]? This question gets less and less veiled and less and less hidden in the depth and complexity of Nietzsche's narration, which is always simultaneously an auto-narration—in my opinion, this particular philosopher was never engaged in anything other than self-knowledge. The question comes out of the depths, closer and closer to the surface, leading Nietzsche to more and more explosive themes which culminate in a kind of *coming out* in his arguably most insane philosophical auto-narrative project: *Ecce Homo*. He certainly had considered the question of the birth of human subjectivity and its moral genealogy earlier: "I do not think there has ever

---

18 F. Nietzsche, *The Genealogy of Morality*, trans. C. Diethe, Cambridge University Press 2006, p. 24.

been such a feeling of misery on earth, such a leaden discomfort". This is how Nietzsche sums up his exposition of how the "wretched man" became "an animal capable of making promises". He continues this genealogy of subjectivity in a manner which in principle already makes him a psychoanalyst: "And meanwhile, the old instincts had not suddenly ceased to make their demands!"—of course it is again all about self-psychoanalysis. "But it was difficult and seldom possible to give in to them: they mainly had to seek new and as it were underground gratifications. All instincts which are not discharged outwardly turn inwards—this is what I call the internalization of man: with it there now evolves in man what will later be called his 'soul'. The whole inner world, originally stretched thinly as though between two layers of skin, was expanded and extended itself and gained depth, breadth and height in proportion to the degree that the external discharge of man's instincts was obstructed... All those instincts of the wild, free, roving man were turned backwards, against man himself."[19]

This is an ultra-Freudian vision of anthropogenesis as a cruel self-aggression of man who, torn out of the state of nature, must contain his drives and direct their power against his own innocence, thereby creating himself in the deeper sense—civilization and its discontents. The easy association with the bourgeois cliché of the "return to naturalness and vigor" suggested by the phantasmagoria of the "race of conquerors and masters" aside, here one can also find a hidden answer to the most private and shameful question (of course, we know it from Nietzsche himself that philosophy comprises exclusively of private and usually shameful questions): Is it possible that my neurasthenic fragility and sickliness, my pains and ailments, my maladaptation to the world which surrounds me, my bitterness, my anger, my pathos and my pathology, all stem from an excess of consciousness, from hypertrophy of contemplation and surplus of sophistication? This is supported by the fact that the subsequent extensive portrait of man's identity is undoubtedly, and perhaps exclusively, a self-portrait: "Man, full of emptiness and torn apart with homesickness for the desert, has had to create from within himself an adventure, a torture-chamber, an unsafe and hazardous wilderness – this fool, this prisoner consumed with

---

19 Ibid., p. 57.

longing and despair, became the inventor of 'bad conscience'. With it, however, the worst and most insidious illness was introduced, one from which mankind has not yet recovered; man's sickness of man, of himself."[20] However strange these enunciations may sound, not long after, psychoanalysis will officially and scientifically proclaim that man is a creature sick from itself by nature. Of course, this will be done in a different idiom and with a different vocabulary—the Nietzschean one was ultimately too exalted and antimodernist in too elitist a way. This sheds even more light on the evidently self-therapeutic nature of Nietzschean truths: they are above all truths for the sake of the author himself, his better comfort in the face of the horror and misery of his existence.

Here we have reached the very epicenter of Nietzschean ambivalence, the principle trait of his entire philosophy whose importance is hard to overstate. Nothing provides as many ambivalent feelings as an ongoing attempt to estimate oneself, to measure one's own "power", to recognize one's significance for humanity. Toward the end of his long argument, Nietzsche suddenly falls into an unexpected awe in a manner typical of bipolar personalities: "Since that time, man has been included among the most unexpected and exciting throws of dice played by Heraclitus' 'great child', call him Zeus or fate—he arouses interest, tension, hope, almost certainty for himself, as though something were being announced through him, were being prepared."[21] And so the sick, suffering and tortured animal is after all sublime and beautiful—not despite, but because it is sick. Nietzsche was perhaps too ambitious and delicate toward himself to leave behind a cryptic self-portrait without a few warm words of deserved (self) love and at the same time too chimeric and witty not to equip it all with a disarming preface which bears all the marks of one written after the work and which claims emphatically, perhaps in order to distance itself from its own veiled confessions, that: "We are unknown to ourselves, we knowers: and with good reason. We have never looked for ourselves, – so how are we ever supposed to find ourselves?"[22]

---

20 Ibid., p. 57.
21 Ibid., p. 57.
22 Ibid., p. 3.

Quite contrary to the tricky camouflage, which as a typical Nietzschean falsetruth should not lead us into the trap of consequential thinking ("oh, so this is all just some insignificant imagination, after all he says, he does not know anything about himself"): Nietzsche never did anything but "seek himself", in a more or less veiled way, since one can "seek oneself" by writing anew the prehistory and history of man (alas, only such a quest after oneself may make any sense). An open explosion of the mania "over oneself" takes place in Nietzsche precisely when he decided, perhaps in an attempt to use this psycho-immunizing measure to defend himself from his immanent nervous breakdown, to carry out a radical self-declaration and self-constitution as the ultimate genius of fitness. This intention found its realization in *Ecce Homo*, whose subtitle is *How One Becomes What One Is*. The work consists of answers to several famous questions which represent the most impertinent, insolent and daring variation on the ancient slogan Know Thyself to be found in the history of philosophy. These questions, posed without a question mark are: "Why I am so wise"; "Why I am so clever"; "Why I write such good books"; and "Why I am a destiny".[23] As is well known, this is not a reading for those who are easily embarrassed in the face of a shameless self-denudation of pride and even less so for those who cannot see in this arch narcissism something at once humorous and fragile, genuinely delicate and touching. But even if someone wanted to view it as simply a fit of psychotic self-adulation they would still have to take note of the fact that soon after writing those words Nietzsche will, allegedly, use his own body to protect a horse from the owner's brutal whip in Turin—his nerves were at that time at the highest tension and sensitivity. Besides, this self-adulation is also a self-ridicule, an invitation to mockery, a kind of quietly experienced cheerful martyrdom against the pillory of social contempt, if not all the worse, pitiful disregard whose discreet and absolutely private sweetness is known to anyone who ever floated in the cloud of radical reclusion and contemptible severance from *our daily bread*. Earlier and in a more embryonic and ambivalent form, this was the meaning of his monstrous moustache, something on the verge of pride and self-parody. By covering his entire mouth, it deformed his face and robbed it of its organ of speech; it closed "the windows and

---

23 F. Nietzsche, *Ecce Homo*, trans. R. J. Hollingdale, Penguin 1992.

doors"; it said that it has nothing to say. It is curious that, as far as I know, Nietzsche's moustache never became an object of philosophical reflection as if we all pretended that it never existed even though it is a well-known fact that philosophers have always paid much attention to their appearance—nothing is coincidental in that department, not the coarse tunic of Diogenes, not Spinoza's coat with its hole from a stabbing etc.

Nietzsche's moustache is no ordinary standard moustache; its function is much deeper and almost revolutionary with regard to the "normal" gesture of the handlebar moustache. It is true that during Nietzsche's time abundant stubble was the norm and so his moustache could have appeared to the inattentive as unimportant and simply in need of a trim. Typically, a moustache is meant to emphasize and sharpen facial features, to make it appear larger, to give it authority and a warrior motif: it is a mark of battle, a mark of flamboyant masculinity. At first glance it may seem that such is its function for Nietzsche too—it is enough to imagine him without it. And yet there is some exaggeration in it, some "trick", something is not quite right here, someone is "playing a different game". This moustache covers, as we have already noted, almost the entire mouth, turning the face into a mouthless mask; it must have been extremely inconvenient when eating as well (maybe there is a connection between this and his ascetic diet, forced upon him by gastric problems). This unkempt moustache also marks a kind of nonchalance and carefreeness which, however, has nothing to do with abnegation. In fact, the moustache is neat and one can speak of no sloppiness here. In a way, it seems to "question" the entire face and to "rob it": it seems to cover, to destroy the contours, to disorient the enemy—such a moustache is never worn "by accident". Rather, the aim is to bring the face to the verge of the current facial regime, to the extreme of the self-unmasking which is still somehow masked. Perhaps it was the most risky, caricature and provocative jester moustache which Nietzsche could afford in his life journey through the margins of the bourgeois world in which he did belong, socially, but not mentally. It was moustache-ridicule of the regime of masculinity and "Germanic-ness" as well as the ancient tradition of *kalokagathia*—with such a moustache the face consciously becomes a provocation to be slapped and held in contempt, especially by such "serious gentlemen" as Wagner. It almost becomes the face of an idiot, with his blank stare: peculiar, strange and "terrible". Nietzsche knew the art of *losing face*, facelessness, due to which what looks at you from the other side of the mirror is an abyss. *Ecce Homo* repeats entirely and radically this gesture of self-loss through self-caricature.

One cannot avoid mentioning the fact that Nietzsche the Philosopher was also a decided opponent of modernity, a classic "anti-modernist", who held the fundamental values of the Enlightenment, reason, democracy, egalitarianism, utilitarianism and civilization in contempt. He was not interested in technology and only respected science in his own idiosyncratic way and for his own revolutionary and perverse purposes. He considered the modern to be an obstacle to human self-knowledge which, in his project, was supposed to combine the most intensive self-contemplation with the maximum of self-creation, all fundamentally in the spiritual and individual dimension. Thus Nietzsche seems to be a perfect guru for all those who are alienated from actuality, for idio-utopians and the fanatics of the antiquated—technology, the maid of comfort, laziness and ergonomics, is not their goddess; on the contrary, in various critical theories, it often turns out to be one of the main forms and central mechanisms of repression, barbaric practices and false consciousness. Although inspired by evolution, Nietzsche, as a critic of his times, had to provide an account of the moral devaluation, decadence and nihilism which were then prevalent as well. Perhaps ultimately, one cannot treat Nietzsche seriously unless one notices in him another emblematic incarnation of modern man: Nietzsche was not just sick from himself, he was also a symptom, or rather an extremely specific dramatization of the more general panhuman crisis and disenchantment, a more or less aware sense of decline which constitutes the consciousness of mature modernity, not only demystified but also disillusioned with itself. It is obvious that Nietzsche was a strictly modern philosopher regardless of the fact that he viscously attacked "modern ideas". As a superhumanist he has a precursor already in Pico della Mirandola and his foundational modern declaration of the limitlessness of human nature which is capable of being equal to gods, from *De hominis dignitate* (1486). Superhumanism has always secretly accompanied humanism. The Nietzschean philosophical project should therefore be ultimately understood pessimistically, as the deepest and perhaps most beautiful articulation of the euphoric-agonal phase in the history of modern man: the "übermensch" is the swan song, the harbinger of an end, an expression of maximal exhaustion and convulsive bitterness of the great defeat of the highest flung modern hopes. It is putting on a brave face. Nietzsche is perhaps the first man of the 20th century, the first man of "total stress". He is the man of tension, experienced and generated through his diagnosis, and more so even in his recipes and the requirements which he imposes on himself and humanity at large through his hurray-ambitious projects—all of this can be interpreted as a grimace borne out of overburdening extreme stress of modern existence.

The post-Nietzschean (although not exclusively) motif of the modern scientific-technological civilization as the fall of humanity and human self-knowledge as well as man's most original acquaintance with being will be exploited up until the post-existentialist nausea of Heidegger. It will also be taken up by the critics of the culture industry and mass communication such as the Frankfurt School, Debord and Baudrillard. The fundamental argument in this critique is the unmasking of mass consciousness in its various forms and incarnations, from totally ordered masses to masses which are amorphic and atomized: the stupefied and de-rationalized mass as false consciousness. In one of its principle definitions, stupidity is the inability to know oneself or an entirely false self-knowledge which takes what is good for what is evil and vice versa—the diffusion of precisely this cognitive deficit is mass culture, programmed and intensified by "mass media". It is precisely due to its scientific-technological foundation that modern civilization, somehow unpredictably and without a prior plan, so to say by accident, implies the birth of mass society and mass man—a radical antitype of the enlightenment dream of the rational individual subject. The atomizing and isolating individualization which takes place within massification does not generate any comprehensive reflective formations of personal self-knowledge but instead its "economy" version—fragmentary and helpless trash subjectivity which is steered by the outside and more automatic than autonomous, impulsive-compulsive. The fact that technology alienates man from himself and de-emancipates him is also an element of the Marxian critique, although its eschatological dimension introduces a dialectical reversal of this regularity, since the development of technology ("productive forces") must ultimately lead to the kind of change in social relations where capitalism is no longer possible to uphold. Thus for Marx, technology is a tool of enslavement as much as liberation.

Perhaps the most comprehensive and in-depth study of what the individual and his self-reflection was in the culminating days of advanced mass civilization of mature industrial modernity is Robert Musil's *Man without Qualities*.[24] Musil was a writer with a technical education who abandoned his career as an engineer to pursue literature and who generally turned his back, rightly or not, on the world of civilization for the sake of spiritual reality. This is, in a way, another opposite of Robinson Crusoe—the man without qualities does not know who he is and what he is capable of, nor does he know what his goal is. Clearly, as per the standard program of bourgeois individualization, he ventures to discover who he is—he wants nothing more and nothing less than to know himself, to test himself, to show for himself and to become someone. But in modern society, with its unclear processes and perspectives, vague horizons and indefinite goals, with its dialectic which flips apparently unequivocal things on their heads, this turns out to be impossible both objectively and subjectively. The reason is that irony and scepticism do not allow the individual to identify with anything determined by the degenerate culture, which ultimately leads one to transgressive and ecstatic-mystical searches—one more paradox of the catastrophic individualism of the man without qualities. Although this is one of the most impressive explorations of the inner world of an individual in the history of literature and at the same time an account of a journey of consciousness toward higher and higher states of spiritual initiation and reconciliation, it ultimately fails to answer the question of who both Ulrich and man in general are. Even more, it shows why and for what specific reasons, due to what specific factors, an answer to this question cannot be obtained at all. It also offers a detailed study, cast in the context of various cognitive dispositions (the perspective of the work oscillates between the dry realism of an empirical-behavioral description and symbolic-imaginative fantasy, between derisive vivisection and delighted and exalted elevation, between chill and ecstasy), of the conditions of this impossibility. It presents an unfinished history and philosophical documentation of how the figure of modern man embodied by Ulrich, with his education, formation and self-consciousness on the highest level of individual development—not an everyman but also not a superhero, more like a man-idea or a protagonist type—seeks "unity lost". However, this search takes place within a broken culture and a world

---

24 R. Musil, *The Man without Qualities*, trans. S. Wilkins, Vintage Books 1996.

without form and purpose in which sensible and well-educated subjectivity discovers one more dimension of immanent limitlessness: the limitlessness of the element of stupidity with its awesome fertility and ingenuity.

This is why the figure of the man without qualities, sketched with lines bereft of contour, with its indefiniteness and indistinctness, is perhaps the most mature and furthest going problematization of modern humanity. Here the question of non-unity, infinity as multiplicity, the limitless becoming— concepts which constitute individuality as part of the modern world—is formulated in the most comprehensive and insightful way as well as in the context of the modern crisis of hyper-dynamism, super-fluidity and discord with the spirit of the times: spiritual shortness of breath, in short, the common triumph of dullness and insensitivity. Musil's work, which is unfinished and in the second part consists of a multiplicity of fragments whose sequence is not clearly established, is perhaps the last attempt for an absolute synthesis of what is individual, given the potential of modernist literature and mature, maybe even overripe, modernity. It is another all-inclusive phenomenology of the absolute, although one focused on the concreteness of an individual man who ventures to know himself. It strikes one that, due to its synthetic character, *The Man without Qualities*, as far as the intellectual dimension is concerned, is a debate and confrontation of the four "universal first principles" already mentioned above: the ancient principle *know thyself*, the Christian principle *love above all*, the "Eastern" principle *become one with everything*, and the modern principle *break the shackles*.[25] All of these principles enter the stage, confront each other and at the same time transform into each other—ultimately they can all be treated as variants of the same, as four pillars of wisdom, whose conjunction and combination forms an unspeakable principle of all principles. *The Man without Qualities* gives an extensive, piercingly intense and beautiful account of how

---

25 It may be important to note that these principles do not point to any essential concepts of the particular epochs but rather to their colouring—they are not exclusive but merely more or less dominant in their complex composition, much in accord with the idea that by following each other epochs do not erase their predecessors but absorb them. On this account, the modern epoch is certainly the wealthiest and deepest, since in its context each of these principles is thinkable and none gains absolute monopoly.

this conjunction generates the conditions of momentary "altered states", moments of superhuman elevation and a sense of reconciliation. Having become disillusioned with the civilizational project of regaining unity at the level of social politics (which turn out to be fiction, a play of appearances and absurd unpremeditated turns within all collective endeavors), Ulrich turns to the contemplative-physical love of his sister Agatha. He regains the transpersonal and trans-ontic unity in this incestual relationship just to lose it instantaneously due to its impermanence. Indeed, only moments are absolute—in modernity the Faustian problem of momentary perfection is a reversal of the question of the immanent infinity of the individual since, when compared to infinity, finitude plays out in moments and moments are its highest stakes. The entirety of life falls into moments, the impermanent moments of the accelerated flow of time (since, paradoxically and rather maliciously, happiness accelerates the flow of time and misery slows it down), of the faster encroachment of death or the time between those moments: time of routine and boredom. The moments which cut the story of our lives up into an incessant series of endings, micro-terms, little deaths, abandonments, defeats and farewells which remind one over and over again that all that is good ends quickly. However, these moments open up to infinity, to the positive experience of an absolute self-transcendence, the unity with another person, the sense of perfect fullness which infinitely opposes all boredom, which is satiated although energetically tense. Of course, the "journey to paradise" cannot really be anything but an erotic-mystical excursion of lovers to a Mediterranean island, under the burning rays of the sun, to the land of orange groves.

As much as Know Thyself leads the man without qualities to the claim that love is above all, the latter notion moves him toward the ecstatic-transpersonal regions of becoming one with everything and at the same time of self-liberation. However, having crossed all these points and spiritual spaces which they have opened, having completed the journey whose universality is only comparable to – but also so much vaster than – the Dantean journey through Inferno, Purgatory and Paradise, the man without qualities will not remain at the heights of ecstasy since, according to the modernist principle of "quick end" (which is helplessly besieged by the fairy tale formula: they lived happily ever after), the fall and collision with negativity is inevitable and negativity also has the last word. This is why the incestual lovers, having experienced an archetypal shiver in the materialized principle of the reunification of both halves, must leave their happy island. And Ulrich, much like another great protagonist of that time and the history of "self-knowledge" in general, Hans Castorp from *The Magic Mountain*, ultimately goes to war, the First World War, the pivotal point at which mature (or overripe) modernity and the West begin to roll into the abyss.

7. Evolution and Zoodicy: The Animality of Modern Man

The question of the animal origin and animality of man, first brought to the fore by the Theory of Evolution, certainly extends back earlier than the Darwinian turn—the questions of what it means that man is also an animal and what animality is have always been fundamental for human self-understanding. However, evolution changes the configuration of elements from vertical to ultimately horizontal (although with an upward slope). Instead of the old fashioned supremacist structure of God-man-animal, another conception turns out to be more adequate: the development of animal into man, the humanization, the evolution of humanity itself, the intermediate links between the animal and the human, the ultimate blurring out of the boundary separating them. Evolution shows definitively that the difference is fluid and vague and that it is about quantity not quality. Ultimately, the only quality which still appears to distinguish man relatively sharply is the trait of "individuality", although Dolphins have also developed a rudimentary notion of individuation and some minimum of self-consciousness, which suggests that individual self-consciousness may also only be a matter of the degree of development of the brain and mind. Incidentally, this recently (the beginning of 2014) resulted in granting dolphins the status "non-human persons" in India—an event which heralds relatively important changes in the latest trends in human self-knowledge, apparently inclined to negotiate more and more with the animal party, the kind of negotiation which is especially lively in the context of *animal studies*. The opening of a space of communication with animals may be one of the less finished areas of human self-knowledge and the possible path of its future development.

The pre-modern understanding of animality was ambivalent. On one hand, the animal does not have the "knowledge of good and evil", on the other, it is the animality of the body that opens up the dimension of sinfulness and temptation in man—animality is impure. The image of the animal wavers between sentimental sympathy for dullness, insensitivity and lack of reason coupled with silence, and contempt for the cruel, aggressive, predatory and unbridled beast. Evolution ultimately renders animality innocent;

it is a secular and naturalistic "theodicy" (or perhaps "zoodicy" since it is about the nature of the animal and not God): does "evil", in this case predation, not serve the purpose of the purification of being from what is "maladapted" and "harmful"? Dullness too turns out to be doubtful—that animals are intelligent was known way before Darwin, already Montaigne and later Hume had important and anthropologically significant insights regarding the continuum of nature and man. This evolutionary absolution of predation and the cruelty of life also gives rise to ethical programs aimed at individual morality (let us tentatively name them after one of their supposed proponents "Nietzschean") as well as politics. The latter aspect, much connected with international relations, takes the form of political realism and nationalism. Cruelty as the essence of life, an enhancement and natural selection, will now become morally positive, although it may be worth noting that they had always been sought after and so the Nietzschean call does not regard the enhancement of cruelty as much as it does the disposal of hypocrisy and impure conscience. Since everyone must fight for their own share and will get as much as he victoriously claims, predation becomes a virtue. At the same time, this notion, which represents a re-evaluation of animal aggression and instinct, goes hand in hand with the new sinlessness: the acquittal of man as an entity and as an individual who, thrown into the thick of the struggle for survival, does its best and has every right to it, as has been clearly articulated by Hobbes. After all, we all do what we can and what is in our power in order to stay alive. This behaviour is in principle and by nature innocent, beyond good and evil—there is no "original sin", no guilt of existence and no fault for the fact that one is. One of the ancient moral problems of humanity which modern evolutionary science resolves is precisely this: it provides the ultimate and valid acquittal of being, it proclaims beyond all doubt that man is innocent and sinless, that he can do whatever happens to be within his power. This very verdict is what Nietzsche wanted to give a full account of, including its most terrifying consequences—if man is innocent, he can do anything. This is a radicalized formula of the slogan well known from Dostoyevsky: "Without God, everything is permitted". Not only permitted but also all well and good; one needs but to unleash the "will to power" to liberate the life force from under the yoke of the nihilistic Christian virtues which are hostile to being in its essence etc. However, the question remains of whether this acquittal is efficient and brings any relief to man. Can the liberation from impure conscience—this worm which feeds on life, as is suggestively and very persuasively presented by Nietzsche—really make anyone better and stronger? It is obvious that this idea will be forever haunted by the question of the extent to which it justifies real barbarity. Perhaps the fundamental sense of guilt is what can save man… from himself.

Evolution leaves yet another practical question open: what is the essence of the evolution of humanity? Is it a continuation and intensification of natural evolution, an unleashing of its energy? Or is it a deviation from it? Not an intensification but, to the contrary, a mitigation of the conditions imposed by the "state of nature", an inhibition or blocking of at least part of the most undesirable processes? One may say that this is one of the fundamental political issues of not only the 20th century; it remains unresolved and continues to inform the main ideological disputes of our times as well—in this sense we are all still the children of Darwin. Recent scientific discoveries appear to indicate new directions in the understanding of evolution which somewhat alleviate the overtones of classical Darwinism, especially as applied to Social Sciences. The value of altruistic, non-standard, non-aggressive and cooperative behaviors is being uncovered as well as a generally improved perspective on the success and flourishing of societies constrained by inter-individual rivalry. On one hand, evolution still represents the model of scientific explanation in popular consciousness which is evidenced by how often the explanatory schema of the type "this is so because this characteristic of our prehistoric ancestors was promoted by evolution" is used and how willingly it is accepted as conclusive and in no need of further explanation. The fact that evolution is the target of the foot soldiers of the most extreme and anti-enlightenment ultra-conservative groups only adds to its authority—there can be nothing more serious than what the fanatics hate. On the other hand, not everything about evolution is worth defending from the fanatic, at least not all of its interpretations. The theme of predation and cruelty understood as essential and "adaptive" characteristics of life as such has become especially irritable and graceless after the Second World War—if there is something in the intellectual or poetic sphere which is impossible "after Auschwitz" it is the moral affirmation of absolute cruelty and the idea of "selection". For some, this amounts to a "scandalous dilution of our ways" while for others, the progress and moral advancement of man, although what is at stake here is mostly appearances and not the real practice or disposition—no insurance company would be keen to issue any nation a policy for genocide for the next 50 years. The human tendency toward aggression and, if need be, and sometimes needlessly, toward bloodthirstiness seems to have been proven by man more irrefutably than anything else. And what to do with it in light of the evolution of man is a question which evolution itself cannot answer. Science usually resolves certain "human" issues as much as it opens up new irresolvable problems and novel questions which man must somehow answer for himself. What should or can we expect from people at their best if not "the dilution of our ways", if not some minimum of humanity understood precisely as an attempt to slow down the rate of "selection", natural or otherwise, and not its acceleration?

Ultimately, if evolution brings about any "humiliation" of humanity, this is not done through an insistence on continuity with the animal, but in Dawkins's "Selfish Gene". In the discussion of egoism, this theory marks an entirely new hand—we are more likely and quick to accept the fact that man is egoistic than that the proper subject of our egoism is the gene and that it is its interest and welfare which ultimately guides us. This offers an interesting closure to the debate over the proper "natural intentions" or dispositions of man.

8. Modernity as False Consciousness

Modernity, like no other epoch in world history, is characterized by the fact that science and technology significantly determine humanity and the self-understanding of man. This is perhaps most salient in the recognition that the ultimate truth of humanity and the dominant perspective on it have turned out to be materiality, biology and carnality. The modern era is the history of how reason abandons the metaphysical interpretation of being and discovers being as what is natural—it creates scientific inquiry and develops technology. The principal message of enlightened modernity, in terms of human self-knowledge as well as practice and self-emancipation, is that man is a living/material entity. Evolutionary-Nietzschean vitalism is a form of radical materialism. Another form of materialism understood as a specifically modern science is Marxism. For several good reasons, Marxism should not be readily dismissed in the debate over the slogan Know Thyself, which only appears not to be subversive or dangerous for the status quo.

When it comes to the relationship between science and technology seen as products of human labour on one hand, and man himself and human nature, on the other, Marxism enriches the modern worldview with a new perspective: the view from below, from the lowest of the low, from the level which for Plato and many other philosophers was always the bottom rung of being, hardly perceivable from the heights of free thought, the view which unmasks and compromises these heights by asking about their proper material possibility conditions and by disavowing their derived character and their detachment from real processes.

The Marxian unmasking regards one of the deepest truths of modernity and one of the highest postulates of the bourgeoisie in its emancipatory-progressive incarnation: that labour makes one free. Perhaps no other epoch exalted human labour as the source of value more than modernity—its clearest example is Hegel's analysis of the "relationship between master and slave". Frequently commented on and critiqued, it was meant as an intellectual or conceptual "abolition of slavery", a gesture of good faith insofar as Hegel idealistically believed in the absolute supremacy of thought ("being is thinking"). For Hegel, conceptual emancipation is thus more fundamental than the physical one: it is *well known* to all idealists that slavery is first and foremost an attitude. The abolition of slavery is a specifically modern event—no other epoch could even dream of it. Ever since man understood that the value generating power of labour, which not only reproduces and repeats but also produces and multiplies (hence the dynamic of capitalism), he also understood that slavery can be abolished since the power of an increase in labour efficiency will ultimately generate enough wealth for all to be free from miserable existence. Slavery does not stem from ill will but from the fact that if someone is supposed to be free from labour someone else must be enslaved and labour "for two". And as long as labour efficiency is low, the labourer will inevitably meet with radical deprivation and have to live at the lowest possible level of subsistence and utility. However, an increase in productivity allows one to think about labour as capable of lifting that necessity and therefore of liberating the slave from misery and captivity, of making him into an "autonomous" worker. Hegel distilled this concept to a sheer dialectic idea but the principle remains the same: labour abolishes the relationship of master and slave and makes the slave autonomous. Incidentally, for Hegel, the one who transcends the slave relationship and who is the effect of this emancipation ultimately turns out to be the Stoic. The Stoic who always "whether in shackles or on the throne" remembers that the essence of being is the spirit and that spiritual strength far surpasses any natural force and is its source—indeed slavery and everything in general boils down to the proper spiritual attitude for the Stoic. This is precisely where Marx enters the stage with his radical dialectic of bourgeoisie and proletariat which shows how alienated Hegel was even though he managed to sniff out the right traces—Marx stands Hegel on his head. Stoicism is no method of emancipation, not in modernity which marks a real material growth as opposed to ancient stagnation.

Marx's response is the following: quite against the fact that labour, as an essential human activity, should in principle lift man to better welfare and that it is the essence and proper nature of humanity, it is also dialectical and turns into its own opposite: it alienates itself and thus becomes alienated. And so it is not the slave who turns into his opposite in modern capitalist society but labour which through this reversal robs man of what is human—it dehumanizes him and brings him misery and "stupefaction", degeneration and humiliation. What is most human transforms into what is most inhuman.

Thus, modernity and enlightened humanism, along with their egalitarianism, become compromised as epochs where man is not yet.

"Man is not yet!"—since that this slogan accompanied young Marx (and Engels), Marxism fundamentally always remained a radical superhumanism and an important modern variant of the reception and reinterpretation of the ancient call Know Thyself (the other more right-wing faction within radical humanism would perhaps be Nietzsche and his own slogan: "Man is not enough"). The fact that *man is not yet* compromises the Enlightenment which appealed principally to man and sought its legitimation in anthropocentrism, boasting of it in the face of all theocrats and orphans of God our Lord (who in modernity was forced by rebellious burghers and disoriented plebs to drop the title Lord and become simply citizen god). On the other hand, *man is not yet* sounds utopian, which must have made Marx especially uncomfortable. This is why he will gradually shift from the humanistic unmasking of the alienation of modern man to an analytic-empirical description of the mechanisms and phenomena of capital as such. The discovery of false consciousness nonetheless turns out to be key (on the subject of the critique of false consciousness, Marx is again rivaled only by Nietzsche, and Nietzsche only by Marx). False consciousness implies that an individual can err not only from time to time but pervasively, regarding most if not all of his concepts of the world, people and himself, and live in complete illusion. He can believe in false images veiling the nature of things which is ultimately suffering, the misery of the majority. And as long as it lasts, no individual human consciousness can be truly and genuinely itself, there cannot be fully developed humanity, no spirit—although Marx does not use the last term, one of the obvious observations regarding human alienation from human nature is that alienated people seem at first glance to be dispirited, they are so oppressed and exploited that they become "dull", "subjugated", "helpless" and "barbaric".[26] In practice, false consciousness also consists in that it distinguishes the labourer from the slave and presents him as an allegedly emancipated slave. However, this notion of freedom is itself an alienation since the situation of the labourer, despite conceptual difference, is no better: "His work is not voluntary but imposed,

---

26 1844 manuscripts.

it is forced labour... and man flees from it like from the plague."[27] As far as the general paradigm is concerned, what posed as the dethroning of God and the declaration of the rule and rights of man (no longer given by God but natural and innate) was in fact just a change on the throne. The regime of domination and subjugation has not ceased to exist but merely changed uniforms: God our Lord was replaced by Capital which is an objectified and absolutely alienated human labour, the power of humanity, its commonly generated value, commodified and transformed into an instrument of the depreciation of man (one may say that Marx's evolution is somewhat reminiscent of the journey of those who arrive at the conclusion that trivialities need to be ignored and what is really important needs to be entertained: the infinity, in this case capital and the religion of capitalism). Alienated human labour in the form of capital becomes power which, although human, evades man and becomes his God—and the true one, for that matter, one which can really determine the lot of humans and subjugate man to its brutal whims and arbitrary instability, its wild element: the analysis of commodity fetishism in *Capital* is an unmasking of how capital magically transforms material objects into commodities whose transactional value seems to stem naturally—this is precisely the role of fetishization—from its use value. Capitalism is new theology.[28]

By unmasking false consciousness, Marx says what will also be said in an epigrammatic nutshell by perhaps the first modernist proletarian poet, Rimbaud: I am someone else. I am not myself, I am still a slave, modernity has deceived us and still does.

This critique certainly does not cancel my individual "I", although by uncovering its social conditioning it questions its autonomy, sovereignty and efficacy. Mature modernity, where Marx undoubtedly belongs, differs from the classical modernity of Hegel in that it questions all the "master" qualities of the subject: his rule over himself, his influence on himself and on his destiny and environment, and finally his rationality and self-evident orientation toward the good (which was still uncontroversial for the Enlightenment: only the Marquis de Sade, or someone like him, could have a laugh at it). It shows how much the subject is an effect, tool, fiction and program,

27 Ibid.
28 See K. Marx, *Das Kapital*, Aristeus Books 2012, pp. 27–32.

to what degree he is not in his own hands but in the hands of more power-ful processes. At the same time, the "I" is the main value which needs to be reinstated, the ultimate goal of the movement of becoming—in this respect Marx simply follows Hegel: alienation somehow marks a transitional stage, its concept contains the suggestion of reversal, the spirit of the boomerang. And at the end there will take place the abolition of negativity: "the libera-tion of each particular individual".[29] But perhaps the concept of alienation is no less illusory and deceptive than the concept of individual conscious-ness—the suggestion that it is negativity may easily lead one astray and to the allegedly obvious claim that it is "untruth" and thus that it must become its opposite. Dialectics may be, despite all its subtlety, too speculative to grasp the gist of the matter which is more complicated than the simple transfigura-tions offered by the dialectization of the problem. This is because dialectics imposes the thought that since *man is not yet*, he is bound to come. Perhaps this construction is still overly idealistic.

---

29 Marx and Engels. German Ideology.

9. Technology and the Mind, God-Machine, The Individual vs. Facebook

He who knows himself in a modern way faces three great riddles: the mystery of the body; the mystery of the mind; and the mystery of the "I". These are the three fundamental orientation points of self-knowledge and self-understanding and science can supply them with a common denominator in the form of empirical explication, although with various degrees of success. We know a lot about the body and much less, and less clearly so, about the "I"; we know more and more about the mind. We also know that, in some sense, they are identical: the body is the mystery of the mind and the mind is the mystery of the "I". The "I" is also related to the multiplicity of minds and thus the multiplicity of bodies and community. If so, there are ultimately only bodies and they are the proper object of our knowledge. And yet what does this actually mean, what is the exact purport of this identity? Despite all reductions, does some kind of dualism not provide the necessary tool for a description of what is subjective and thus impossible to be made into an "object"? Of course, this does not mean that dualism can successfully convince us about immortality—nowadays, in the era of late modernity, this conviction seems to be an especially rare grace.

Scientific inquiry into the mind rested at the center of interest of modernity from its very inception and it would be difficult to deny its progress and findings which have significantly shaped our self-conception. Recently, cognitive neuroscience has appeared as the avant-garde of the materialistic conception of the mind and intelligence and their study in experimental terms. This domain's discoveries and achievements can be added to the list of "great humiliations" of humanity, right next to the Copernican, Darwinian and Freudian turns—is the last exclusively human competency, intelligence and thought, not humiliated by every bit of evidence that thinking can be reduced to a program and computer simulated, that specific intellectual functions can be modeled as machine functions, however abstract, in short, that the mind is simply a complicated computer (although not one with serial processing akin to computer processors but one which uses parallel distributed processing)[30]? The riddle of the mind also leads to the old question of whether I am a physical entity or a metaphysical one—and this issue is not ultimately resolved by science, although the more science approaches the mind, the more it demystifies its last mysteries, including those which used to irrevocably demand supernatural provenance. On the other hand, neurology introduces its own dimension of infinity: the infinity of the complexity of the brain which is described by numbers beyond the reach of any human mathematical imagination: "If we assume, conservatively, that each synaptic connection might have anyone of ten different strengths, then the total number of distinct possible configurations of synaptic weights that the brain might assume is, very roughly, ten raised to the 100 trillionth power, or $10^{100,000,000,000,000}$. Compare this with the measure of only 10^{87} cubic meters standardly estimated for the volume of the entire astronomical universe. Each individual human is a unique hand dealt from this monumental deck."[31] Transcendence breathes with huge numbers and so it is no wonder that contemporary philosophy of mind is the keeper of the last strands of the debate on metaphysics.

The fundamental assumption of modernity and the principle of the self-understanding of modern man is technology as the extension and intensification of human capacities—technology is an expansion of the human body and its possibilities, and in this sense it changes the essence of humanity. The latter went through several significant self-requalifications in its modern history: from a flightless animal to an animal capable of flight, from one whose life expectancy is around 40 to one that dies around 70, from a population of 100,000,000 to the current 7 billion, etc. As such, technology is an anthropomorphization of the environment, its "humanization", an adjustment of nature to human needs. Paradoxically, the furthest going technological humanization of the environment frequently turns into something most inhuman, not only on the occasion of great anthropogenic natural catastrophes (oil spills, nuclear disasters, etc.) but also where the scale and degree of brutality with which technology transforms nature

---

30 P. M. Churchland. *The Engine of Reason, the Seat of the Soul: A Philosophical Journey into the Brain*, MIT Press 1996, p. 11.
31 Ibid., p. 5.

brings about, due to its artificiality, the shiver of natural opposition, a physiological fear (anything from strip mines to plastic surgery).

It is no wonder that this fear turns into panic at the mention of a technical-instrumental extension onto the machine of what is most human: intelligence. The "age old" myth of the modern world has been Frankenstein and other "androids" spun out of control. The fear which inhabits this myth was additionally fueled in the second half of the twentieth century by the scientific-technological quest for artificial intelligence which is still far from over but is nonetheless not entirely devoid of important effects, not only side effects. This may be the ultimate and unsurpassable feat in the history of human self-knowledge—here the subject and the object truly become absolutely the same as the brain knows itself both theoretically and in practice when it makes a copy of itself, an artificial substitute, as proof of its utmost creative capacity. By adding to it the theory and practice of genetic engineering we open up an immense field of limitless post and trans-humanistic innovation whose unbound power is the newest object of faith, hope and love for contemporary technophiles and technocrats who still find the source of quasi-religious or existential inspiration in the "potential of human creativity" taken as the panacea for all "human troubles"—in order to observe this, it suffices to take a look at the euphoric aura accompanying presentations in the TED cycle and the burning effect it has on its overenthusiastic believers.

According to this line of reasoning, only now do we stand at the threshold of a truly intelligent era—the new smart world with all its unbound potential for development which is yet to open up before us. And although the holy grail of this cause is "an artificial person", or at least a machine capable of passing the Turing Test (the idea, in short, is that a computer manages to deceive a human into thinking that it is not a computer but a fellow human, and the question of whether such a perfect imitation would make it "a thinking entity"), the practical results in the field, including those already visible, stem more often from an analytic and functional study of thought processes and the mechanic modeling of its various particular functions: from practical cognitive applications which can subsequently find use in the realization of the vision of an "information society". Several principle inventions functionally converge with many hypotheses and findings in neurology to jointly create the foundations for another turn: the digital revolution whose ultimate sense is not so much what has been foreseen by the humanistic scarecrows such as the "rebellion of intelligent robots". Instead, another direction emerges where computerized and networked technical devices know more and more—at least in the sense in which to know is to remember and be able to somehow actively use memory, to "process"—and appear beside man as the "smart devices" which know much about and for him. And how does that impact human self-knowledge?

Ever since the existence of knowledge and its recording, the fundamental and practical issue of science has been its preservation and storage—technical limitations might never have been more severe and difficult to overcome than in this field and nowhere else did revolution occur so late. It is true that the invention of print was ground breaking but the genuine breakthrough only took place with the miniaturization of information storage over the last twenty years, beginning somewhere in the 1990s, along with the accompanying digitalization of resources due to which all forms of knowledge—text, image, film and sound—can be transformed into "files" transferable between multiple material carriers and players. They can also be sent via the internet and even stored there, replacing all traditional archives, multimedia libraries etc. The digital leap is thus a leap from the domain of an inevitably limited capacity for record keeping, from the realm of the necessity to forget, to the realm of practical infinite memory, of remembering everything—due to miniaturization and the low cost of memory storage coupled with its gigantic capacity (measured in gigabytes prior to 2014 and now more frequently in terabytes), a practically infinite and unlimited amount of data can be stored without the need for much austerity. These changes are altering the very notion of knowledge since its possession and accumulation are ceasing to be exclusively human, at least on the basic level. These devices and apparatuses remember more and more and get better and better at utilizing it, that is, they are becoming more and more adept at the art of ordering content, searching and associating information, recognition, classification and inference. Of course, at the top of each such process there must still be a human who makes this or that decision based on the data received from the analytical apparatus. However, these decisions are also more and more often ceded to automatic instances; even death and life decisions. This means that there is more and more substance which is known and initially analyzed in the name of man by devices equipped with memory (we used to remember the birthdates of our friends and family; now it is remembered for us by our pocket memory devices). This is often knowledge about man himself, intimate and even compromising. Think of what my machines know about me: the "search history", pictures and films I made with my mobile, text messages I have sent and received, online transactions I have made... On board, local and mobile memory devices, as well as various functions for processing the data stored on them, customized for the function of the given device and coordinated with other devices—physical and more frequently virtual—realize the world of knowledge, the world saturated with data, information and their flow which is no longer known to any one man, about which you do not have to think for yourself and which is used at an enormous scale by the intelligent and interconnected equipment all around us. The cyber-prophets have already painted a vision of super-comfortable houses and appliances, cars, planes, communication channels and public spaces of various scale and function which will intelligently adjust to the actual needs of their users, which will learn, make forecasts, minimize costs and maximize the ergonomics of their own use.

Interestingly, there is no need in all of this for the machines to become anthropomorphic or indistinguishable from persons—there are enough authentic "normal" people for this not to be economically justified. The intelligent and networked techno-sphere is developing in a different direction: an omniscient yet impersonal mega-machine which can potentially connect into one device all communicational and audio-visual devices and processors, along the data stored and sent by them, making them mutually associated and available (for example, health data and expense data as well as data related to your career, although stored in different data bases, can in principle be combined). This could also become available to at least some human subjects. The cyber trans-humanist has an idea of who that might be: probably all data processing units starting with virtual espionage and research automata to the meta-analysts who use algorithms and programs for data management to the strategists deciding whether to send off a digital patch... All this can perhaps realize some kind of utopian vision of the society of absolute knowledge, the totally rational world where there exists detailed and objectified knowledge about each individual and each of his actions—a world which is not only ordered and regulated but also capable of thought and learning "in accord with your changing needs" (or perhaps in a grimmer version, changing you "in accord with its needs"?) Be that as it may, it will be a world of total transparency in which, as the CEO of Google Eric Schmidt already said in 2009, "If you do not want something to be known about you, do not do it."[32]

In this technological utopia, customized programs for personal data analysis will inhabit the new intelligent sphere of the extension of the mind and the development, or better, the technicization of subsequent mental functions. These programs will supplant us in thinking and decision making in real time—perhaps a personalized dieting application will choose our meals; a personal trainer will decide about our exercise and instruct us; a mood optimizer will suggest what to do in a given situation in order to feel optimal based on a comprehensive analysis of data ranging from brainwaves to weather forecasts to our daily schedule. One can imagine an unlimited wealth of applications and programs for the analysis of personal data which might make our life much more convenient and free from irritating choices and routine reflections—would it not be wonderful if the fridge ordered the food you needed based on an indepth familiarity with your habits and needs (potential doubts could always be consulted via email) and thereby free you from burdensome chores and give you more time to contemplate something more sublime? These quasi-mental functions will work with the material contained in the individual space of the so-called digital shadow: an individual's data which can be gathered and communicated by personalized intelligent devices, including location, the nature of the environment, electronic transactions and transmissions, physiological parameters, data from personal multimedia devices, audio and video files, links, search histories, browsing histories, clicking histories and other types of activity online and within telecommunication networks, coupled with data from social media and other files, documents and statistics. These streams of data are at the same time also recorded and thus made forever replayable and widely available through the network, if not for all then at least for some. What is significant is that the sphere of autonomous activity of all these devices is too great for the user to be able to monitor or authorize each activity performed by them—many are performed via remote signals originating from external control centers, which means that my direct personal sphere of intelligent

---

32 Cited after *Gazeta Wyborcza* (*The Electoral Gazette*), 24 April 2014.

technical support is also open and susceptible to all kinds of interventions and interference from the outside. This is how this techno-utopia turns into a techno-dystopia.

One of the ground breaking neurocognitive innovations regarding digital technology is the automation of the intellectual function of recognition, including the recognition of select types of objects and most of all facial recognition. This function is important insofar as it touches upon one of the fundamental and at the same time publicly available markers of individuality: the face and its identification. It may appear *prima facie* innocent—computers have learned to do with an effort what small children can do—but the automation of facial recognition in connection with mass monitoring carried out with the help of high resolution cameras and its potential networking allows for the individualization of automatic surveillance on an unprecedented scale. The total network of control may see where you are and what you are doing and even what you are about to do. It may seem too futuristic but technically it is already doable, at least at the level of testing. Moreover, first solutions within an "automatic behavior analysis" are already being implemented with the aim of carrying out the screening of individuals in public places, scanning their profiles etc. One does not have to be an extreme technophobe to worry that what is technically plausible sooner or later will become doable and will be implemented, not necessarily for the greater good—the development of technology is in fact unstoppable.

It is also easy to imagine that the sphere of intelligent daily life mind support will be infiltrated by unauthorized programs derived from the network which will imperceptibly interfere with your thinking, spy on it, embed within it, and ultimately perhaps correct or deform it. Of course, it is far from necessary to picture it emotionally or visualize it in terms of some totalitarian oppression, violence or brutal and repressive violation of individuality. Perhaps in an advanced society based on knowledge, the information society, the society of intelligent and informational devices and networked minds, the formation of individuals and the discreet steering of them will assume imperceptible forms entirely profiled and customized to everyone's fancy— plush and painless, such as those shown in the 2013 film *Her*. This utopian picture whose plot is set in an indefinitely near future in a super-comfortable intelligent techno-sphere, where the impact of the machine on man is in the sphere of intimacy: even today we already know this peculiar intimate bond which forms in the relationship between the "I" and the personal computer and smartphone. However, in the film the operating system has reached the level of complexity proper to a person, which, of course, leads to the question of whether the machine will challenge man, and if so, then how. The charm of this particular picture consists in the fact that it offers a relatively warm and romantic response—the machine will take the place of another human for the man, and then it will dump him for another machine. It sounds sinister but it is ultimately better than an attempt to take power or start another war. But the more general moral is the model of control which the intelligent system of the techno-sphere will exert over an individual—whether it will be smooth and thus perfectly translucent in its totality, characterized by minimum friction and maximum appeal, tempting rather than repressive and controlling.

What will this frictionless society be like: a perfect republic or an absolute tyranny? Or perhaps an ideal regime, the synthesis of both. Will it be a state where the principle Know Thyself has been raised to the level of continuous and systematic surveillance, absolute visibility and total information? Perhaps it will render life error free and the ubiquitous intelligent monitoring will secure us at every step, advise us in each situation and suggest an optimal solution to each of our problems, like a kind of technocratic providence watching over us all at once and each person alone.

A typical question which consistently springs up in the context of scientific research on intelligence and the attempt to model it digitally is whether machines can become persons or people (the Turing Test). In response to it we should note that there is no need for it and that a much more interesting question is: can a machine become God? And can a new version of the Turing Test, TT 2.0, conceptualize the criteria for the recognition of this fact? An omniscient virtual machine, equipped with infinite knowledge and capable of following each individual in real time, of embedding itself in personal applications and of conducting automatic analysis of all personal data—a techno-guardian angel of sorts—could perhaps also come up with its own unique book: the Face Book. The book could provide an initial and relatively significant pool of information about each registered user. An intelligent and self-learning program could process and analyze this data in real time and draw the appropriate conclusions and consequences, hopefully beneficial for us, if we assume "good will" on the part of this godly machine and its industrious trustees. Perhaps such a pan-machine could no longer be denied some kind of subjectivity and intelligence and the entire so-organized system, some kind of new substantiality/personality. Who knows, perhaps at such a level of advancement there could emerge a kind of trans-humanistic logosphere whose subjectivity would realize in its own way, on its own accord and for its own needs, the ancient slogan Know Thyself.

The so-called "social media" is the latest vogue in communication technology combined with the intelligent techno-sphere of devices and minds; it thus constitutes the most current phenomenon in the history of human self-knowledge. Dialogue with oneself is after all a type of communication and even though it appears not to be too susceptible to the influence of technology it is nonetheless its part, the greater the more the subjectivity owes to the network of mind to mind interactions in the context of a growing number and density of connections. The development of communication consists in the densification of the data transmission network and the growth of its bandwidth. Although purely quantitative, this notion leads to qualitative leaps—to growth in complexity, followed by a change in the general conditions of self-identity and subjectivity which are always derived from the various readily available instruments for its formation, representation, publication, confrontation and connection with others. Social media—may they be represented by Facebook, which dominated the market in 2014—are comprehensive and still developing multi-functional tools for the management of social identity: affiliations, relations, roles and social networks characteristic of the individual. The global success of this tool (one billion users worldwide) depends, first of all, on the expansion of the communication network itself and its growing rate of penetration, and secondly, on the fact that it gathers and associates, in one stream of activity and one "place", the transmission of various social functions and facets of social capital, allowing for a simultaneous performance of an identity narration, of who one is, and a reflection in the mirror of other self-narrations (for example, when you are "tagged by user Gillian"). Of course, various strategies of honesty and play, falsity and truth, playfulness and seriousness, triviality and depth, all in differing proportions and variations are possible. Since everyone can post to his profile, and at the same time to the data stream of all his acquaintances, any multimedia or text content, attachment or link (barring the limitations imposed by custom and law), create an "event" and invite whoever he wants from among his friends to it or even make it open for "all users", whether it be landing on Mars or his cat's birthday, everyone can comment on it, like it or ignore it, and the like. Everyone has an unlimited, practically infinite number of options and possibilities to express their identity and to communicate, also with oneself, who he is. Facebook therefore turns out to be a kind of virtual online personal diary and album, as well as a guestbook and photo-archive, a record of all actions and a bank of all social relations within the given individual account. Seen from the objective-epistemological point of view, it is an extremely comprehensive and multidimensional, if somewhat chaotic and fanciful, individual dossier of each "user". From the point of view of the surveillance and invigilation of citizens, it turns out to be a prime instrument of profiling and control—of course, not of particularly dangerous individuals as these are not very likely to advertise themselves on Facebook, although this does not stop the American surveillance apparatus from copying and monitoring the resources stored on private company servers.

10. That which Returns

Despite all the scientific and technological progress, all the changes that have been brought about by it and all the facets of our human civilization that are governed by it, despite all the discoveries and demystifications, breakthroughs and deconstructions, the last of the three great riddles—of body, mind and the self—still remains mysterious and as unsusceptible to the impact of science and technology as ever. It seems that wherever the right conditions for reflexive human individuality arise, albeit exclusive (and regardless of the question of whether there could ever arise social circumstances in which genuine and deep individuality would be denied to no one, as was Marx's ardent belief), there is always some dimension in which it assumes some universally communicable shape and mechanism and some reoccurring form. Perhaps in the space of human individuality, like nowhere else, the truth of all becoming is eternal return: something here is not subject to change across various contexts. This is why we always have the impression that, despite all the differences in time and place, some formulae of self-knowledge are entirely transparent and intelligible to us, that some immutable mechanisms of being-oneself, self-creation and self-contemplation are close by, understandable and within our grasp, even after millennia.

There is nothing in the *Meditations* of Marcus Aurelius, including the first book which is the author's extensive self-presentation, that would not be transparent for us both on the surface and in depth. Of course, there is an extremely clear and specific context there, an entirely unique situation—aristocratic environment, education and political function—which may suggest that there is nothing more remote, hermetic and unintelligible to my perspective as an apartment dweller than the Emperor of Rome: what can I know about being the Emperor of Rome? And yet, I understand him so well and grasp his situation so easily; even more than that, I see through his human, his arch-human tactic which determines his self-description: a long detailed list of his merits, some of which are simple and rather general (to grandpa Verus I owe "decency and a mild temper"), and some more specific and subtle: Alexander the Platonist taught me "rarely, and never without essential cause, to say or write to anyone that I am too busy."[33] For the sake of modesty, it needs to be assumed that all the good in me, this entire sequence of virtues, is owed to others. So let me make a detailed list, along with a subtle description of my merits and advantages, so that I can pay my tribute to all those who passed them on to me: father, mother, forefathers, teachers, friends, gods etc. At the same time, let me indirectly create an exquisite panegyric of myself. *Monumentum Exegendum Est*—I thank them for how perfect I am with a bronze statue of myself as I have the fortune and privilege to be. Modesty, moderation and humility are the three pillars of my perfection. And for a similar reason, to repay this perfection in a pristine way, I will not venture to list my vices. These I owe solely to myself and will therefore be silent on them not to come off as too self-centered.

How human, how arch-human, is this mutual interchangeability of the sense of being unique and perfect (a "genius"; incidentally, at a certain level of social development every man seems to carry in his bag the mace of genius) with the sense of shame and fear of embarrassment, unmasking, susceptibility to being hurt, loneliness and hidden intimidation by the greatness of what is outside, all of which lie in the depths of Marcus Aurelius and explain why he—yes, even he—excluded all his defects, shortcomings and blemishes from his comprehensive picture of himself in an attempt to create an image of an ideal "I". However, would it also not be possible to interpret this self-portrait as an expression of "imperial" thinking, as a construal of oneself which, in its honesty, does not deny its own dominance and mighty perspective, additionally decorated by stoicism and a contemplative-humanistic outlook? Be that as it may, I understand with ease how Marcus Aurelius must have reasoned through the pages of the first book of *Meditations*.

What is at stake here is the question of "genius"—it is this notion, with its romantic connotations, which is perhaps best suited to determine the core of what seems to lay outside the domain of science and technology, in the sphere of absolute individualism. This is the most ungraspable phenomenon and the ultimate problem of an individual man who reflects on himself: something valuable and intimate, fetishistic and narcissistic, proud and at the same time verging on disgrace.

---

33 Marcus Aurelius, *Meditations*, trans. M Hammond, Penguin Books 2006, pp. 1 and 5.

All my biological, social, psychological, cultural and biographical characteristics, all that I will list when they ask me who I am, regardless of context and of how specific and concrete they are meant to be, are general, repeatable and shared with others: they are not exclusively mine or idiosyncratic. All these qualities are universals, each occurs commonly and ubiquitously, sometimes rarely and sometimes more frequently, but never merely in one case and as exclusively one's own, perhaps barring certain protein structures which are individual and unique. All else defies monopoly and cannot be labeled with a proper name, our name. Each individual consists of an infinite number of qualities and traits none of which are uniquely his—uniqueness and specificity lies only in the combination of these elements. Of course, there are so many of these original components and so many variations of them that by being unique only in terms of the combination of general qualities people as individuals still differ from each other so deeply that each provokes shock and reflection on the power of differentiation. Even simplicity can be deep and each complexity is dialectical. In short, there is no need to worry since there is enough material to combine for each individual to be able to be infinitely different and one of a kind.

And yet there is some yearning for a concept of the absolutely unique and inimitable—for that which is not a mere combination but which contains in it "something extra"—for genius, an absolutely singular intelligence. It is obvious that the idea of genius is post-theological and that it carries with it the metaphysics of absolute singularity stolen from God—along several other attributes successfully taken over by man in modernity. This is precisely where the unique principle of modernity lies: man pilfers characteristics previously under the divine monopoly and does so with much success, as opposed to the more tragic Promethean variation on the theme. "Genius" stolen from God is therefore the last residue of theology and the unique magic performed by modern man: the magic of an outstanding individual, the spell of the last sorcerer, the modern "great man". Greatness is always connected with the power of human hierarchy and it ideologically justifies domination; psychologically speaking, it is based on narcissistic megalomania and an equally narcissistic dream (often but not always fulfilled) of being worshiped which is also contained in the individualistic paradigm of humanity. In the public sense, greatness does not require much even if it sometimes turns out to be truly awesome: its social distribution is random, its recognizability unclear and its legitimation problematic and easily challenged. However, greatness is the proper space of a genuine and powerful experience of faith—just like we find it difficult to believe in immortality, it is equally difficult to cease believing in individuality, at least in its minimalistic dimension of bodily separateness, but also in the more sublime order of originality and unique power. Modern man believes in himself, in his individual power and irreplaceable singularity, just like ancient man believed in fate—it is difficult to even imagine something else, something going beyond this framework and paradigm. And thus he ventures to advance in the domain of what is his own, he strives to leave some kind of mark, his own achievement, be it in science, business or the arts. The ultimate horizon of activity here is what the writer Parvulescu, the sub-character in Godard's *Breathless*, says when asked about the greatest ambition of his life: "To become immortal and then to die."

In no other epoch has the question of individual style through which to realize one's originality and uniqueness assumed such fundamental significance. Perhaps it is merely a means of manipulation and social hierarchy based on an immemorial and ever abundant human characteristic: gullibility combined with a tendency to boast. Perhaps it is an elite false consciousness which ultimately justifies inequality, even when it engages in subtle and exclusive apologies of human genius by recognizing it in maladapted individuals, declasses and degenerated social outcasts. After all, greatness cannot be denied to what expresses it. Let us not forget the Nietzschean reminder not to fall into resentment and not to view all inequality and injustice as "evil"—so think the victims. Resentment is a petty attitude which expresses our frustration with our own failures. But are the times not vicious enough for us to have the right to feel victimized, outraged and angry? Perhaps one should not be too easily pacified by this charge, typical for Nietzsche's "tough school", the charge which is in fact moral blackmail: do not denigrate life, it is an attitude proper for the slave! But what if we are in fact slaves? What if, as was put forward by Marx, the ultimate emancipation lies ahead of us and we must humbly acknowledge that we still slave away, that the task of human liberation has not yet been achieved?

Perhaps then faith in human greatness, in an individual genius, is the kind of naïve and noble belief which is not worth refuting even if it cannot be separated from its theological provenance and structure. It is not in conflict with the task of emancipation; on the contrary, the ultimate ideal of emancipation is to enable man's full development. The emancipatory utopia gives everyone an opportunity to be great within the community: "Only the community offers each individual the possibility of comprehensive formation of its inborn capacities; only in the community is personal freedom possible."[34] It is thus not worth it to destroy the notion of individual human genius as false consciousness by means of hard social-economic materialism since it is one of the universal stakes of human liberation, the horizon of the "comprehensive formation of one's capacities". What needs to be understood is that man in general is ingenious.

There is also a phenomenon of unjustified greatness, great generosity, which stands out from the average in the hard sense of the term, and somehow against the logic of the circumstances, regardless of the conditions. It occurs when someone possesses several harmonized talents, capacities and merits, often to an utmost extent. Their subject is usually at first (and second) glance an individual who casts an aura of light around them, who carries something intriguing which one is drawn to recognize, identify and understand out of his mystery, something which breeds jealousy and awe. Such individuals often create entirely unique things based on the principle of individual style—not always but sometimes, individual style can be so unique as to be easily recognized "among the crowd", like when you are driving a car and all of the sudden hear some unknown yet "familiar" piece on the radio and then you realize that it is most probably "something by Mozart". And it usually checks out: such is the mystery of style, that "extra something" due to which one can guess that some composition is by Mozart and cannot be named other than by appeal to his given name. In a moment like that you can only shout, "That is it, 'this' must be Mozart!" In art, and in emotions which we feel when we are in contact with an individual genius of beauty, we sense the "touch of infinity"—this is human immanent infinity, the marvelous spark.

Greatness is not a mere illusion, even if one should not go too far in lifting it up over the ordinary. It is usually—if that can be said about greatness—not far removed from the average, although here we encounter another riddle of humanity which is the span of difference (is it a "gap"?) between humans.

---

34 Marx and Engels. German Ideology.

How much does the most outstanding differ from the commonplace? The question is doubly problematic since it also touches on the scale of possible alienation, conflict and exclusion. Be that as it may, the best conditions for human greatness are those offered by solidarity and so no greatness should veil it or create unbridgeable divides. Solidarity is greatness's moral necessity and convenience—this was already known to and interestingly argued for by Oscar Wilde in the *Soul of Man under Socialism*: nothing is more dandy than socialism.[35] It also makes no sense to determine *a priori* how many people are capable of greatness, and even less so whether anyone is in principle incapable of it or not. If greatness—or rather its moral ideal which can be formulated paraphrasing Kant: "Live as if human greatness were possible!"—needs to be solidarizing and nonexclusive, it must, paradoxically, assume the lowest common denominator model. It must tell its story as open ended, modifiable and multi-cultural—it must be minority oriented, minimalistic, inclusive, pluralistic and largely available, not connected with power, domination and hierarchy. It must be decentralized and non-supremacist or, as John Stuart Mill recommended in *On Liberty*, eccentric.

At the same time, greatness is a riddle for itself in that no one person— perhaps except for the biggest and rarest *born under a lucky star* types— cannot be convinced of his or her greatness. Self-knowledge as an appropriate estimation of oneself is perhaps the most difficult task: how hard it is to come up with a proper measure and decent comparison; how many megalomaniacs there are and how many of those who have not had the chance to blossom; how many overrated ones; and how many underrated! What then can I know about my own merits if all appraisals are changeable and all measures relative? This is one of the obsessions of the civilization of dynamism and becoming, one of the obsessions of modern man forever suspended between rise and fall: self-appraisal. One needs to know what one is worth and so one of the most potentially tormenting questions an individual can ask himself is: am I good enough? Am I up to the challenge? There is also the phantasm of not so much the "great other" as the "greater other"—each of us, whoever he or she is, fears the unknown "even better one" who lurks and who might outclass us in what we think we are best at.

---

35 O. Wilde, *Collected Works*. Wordsworth Edition 1997, pp. 1039–1066.

On the other hand, it is difficult, extremely difficult, to estimate it, and so it often becomes a kind of civilizational disease that we estimate ourselves in a maniacal way, without forgiveness and excuse.

Yet it is ultimately obvious that there is very little in the sphere of self-knowledge which we can know with high probability and clarity. Let us ask, "What is or should be the object of self-knowledge?" And what among it can be known with any certainty, what with more certainty and what with less? The question of identity is a matter of fact: history, ancestry, experience, habits and reactions. Desires. Situational orientation in the world. It is potential: possibilities. Weaknesses. Strengths. Values. The ideal "I". Finally, it is plan and project. Self-interest and one's own good.

Self-knowledge consists of the knowledge of the factual, potential and teleological. The factual can be known relatively well, but it can be misunderstood—let us say I offer support to someone in need and I immediately say to myself, "How generous I am!" This type of false interpretation and unwarranted generalization is very common. The potential, what is possible, "all which is in our power", can also be captured with some probability, although here the risk of truly great error and significant over or under-estimation enters the stage. Finally, when it comes to the proper recognition of one's own good and one's own "best and objective interest", it is extremely easy to be mistaken, and even to commit an irreversible error, especially since we all entertain many mutually contradictory desires, often imbued with unforeseen force and persistence, each of which brings on its own values and interests. When death approaches, the last two factors gradually cease to play any role and so there is much truth in the benign observation that only in the end can one genuinely know who one is. It is equally benign to observe that the adage *it is human to err* is nowhere else as true as in the domain of self-understanding—in all three dimensions of self-knowledge, even the most cautious of us are subject to an unimaginable flood of illusions, fantasies, delusions and misunderstandings. The inter-personal sphere feeds off of these illusions every day. Is it not true that the human condition and self-knowledge is partly constituted—and that part is far from marginal—by self-deception, self-delight, the contemplation of our alleged possibilities and dreams of what we are yet to show and achieve, the pleasure of flattering opinions among our friends, the megalomaniacal conviction of the special weight of our experiences, beliefs and opinions which we force onto others with no repentance: the entire inner theatre of self-deception, illusion, gullible narcissism, bragging and pride. Such is the stupidity of megalomaniacal self-love of which no one can know for sure that he does not suffer—do not we all experience it every day among our fellow humans and in ourselves?

These general markers of the condition of human self-knowledge (which is always necessarily also self-deception, the grand narcissistic theatre of masks and a comedy of errors) seem to be constant and their relationship to science and technology is an extremely complex issue. Better education and a higher level of self-reflection should no doubt correlate with greater cognitive success and greater existential and life fulfillment, although one should not count on any guarantees here. The challenge thus remains rather foggy and it defies parameterization. One does not know precisely what and how to grade here. The research project whose nonchalant objective would be to "know oneself" would never win any contest for a grant.

11. The Death of Death and Late Modern Man

The 19th century was the century of the death of God. The 20th century of the death of man. It may be high time to announce the coming of the 21st century and the death of death. However, the point is not to arrive at the negation of negation, which is an affirmation, but to realize that the formula of breakthrough, of an anthropological turn, which is symbolically and briefly expressed by the notion of "death" is too gross a simplification in a processual and dynamic world where crisis is intertwined with development and growth with degeneration. The concept of "death" is too "grand" in the sense in which Lyotard spoke of grand narratives—it is too compartmental and pretentious not to have to die of exhaustion. The complexity of historical time with its complicated and multi-track course does not allow for such cross-sectional conceptions, especially since they are always accompanied by strong postulates. Meanwhile, everything points to the fact that the principle of "strong demands" has also been exhausted and lost its intellectual appeal: who in our times would like to delegate "great tasks" to man with anthropological hooray optimism when the question of the very survival of civilization is sufficiently difficult?

This may be the starkest paradox: the exhaustion of the formula of an "end" came right when the end of man ceased to be a matter of intellectual history and humanistic ideas and migrated to a much more literal register— to the natural order where the contemporary phase often called the Anthropocene Era appears to be nearing the end of its potential for development, growth and expansion, and since expansion is its essence this end will also mark some kind of end for the entirety of civilization. To what extent will this be a series of stormy events as opposed to slow changes over time? Will there be a moment of acceleration and catastrophic culmination? These are the current proper and timeliest questions about the future of man, questions which brush aside all other "deaths". The hope that current trends and irreversible processes, which are slowly gaining speed and carrying us over newer and newer thresholds in the destabilization of the ecosystem, will cease to exert their power or that someone will hit the breaks (due to conscious human endeavor) is slight. The "end of man" really is approaching—it will be at least a civilizational end of "modern man" and, in the worst case scenario, which ultimately seems less likely than the first, the death of the human species.

However, before one or another catastrophe occurs, life will go on as if nothing is happening and as if "Death"—of God, Man and Subject—never occurred in the cultural paradigm and order. Nothing has happened definitively; everything returns and resurrects, or perhaps it simply lives on as an afterlife. The complexity of what is modern does not allow for any radical breaks; it breaks with breaking and thus submerges us in long-term dynamic processes—and only sometimes do periodic and relative accelerations prompt the astonished eyewitnesses, such as Marx or Nietzsche in the 19th century, to spin visions of the coming "Great Leap" (in this, the language of the Communist Manifesto uses an intriguing, for Communism, notion of a "specter"). By the 19th century it certainly seemed that everything had caught the momentum and was quickly approaching revolution. And yet revolution did not take place, at least not in the shapes imagined by Marx and Nietzsche. They both merely lived to see parodies of these revolutions: as if history, already in its first unfolding, happened as farce and at the same time always left its repetition hanging as an option (repetition as an original?). One may seriously doubt whether the repetition will ever happen since it has turned out that the acceleration is still growing—from our perspective, the 19th century was rather "slow"—and that we are still gaining speed. As is captured by the second principle of dynamics, there is no limit to movement and no end to acceleration (other than the speed of light, of course), and there is only one limit, as in the second principle of thermodynamics: absolute exhaustion.

Perhaps the only thing left to man is to delay his own end in time, which is to say, to live. This way we have achieved a dialectical micro-transformation and come from the "death of death" to life—but life in the minimalistic and non-total sense, to life as a "small narration". The fact that life is simply delaying the end is one more truth which has been "sensed since time immemorial" and which appears to be variously confirmed by science and technology. At the same time, this truth is undoubtedly in a value conflict with the earlier postulate of striving for greatness. We seem to face a dilemma: minimalism or maximalism, either or. But it needs to be reconciled. The death of death is actually no "event", it is not enough to "launch a career" since it is in fact the death of an event as positivity. Instead, it is the return of what had been repressed by modernity (as the enlightenment) when it believed that it had managed to negate the negative. A kind of dissolution of modernity in its late stage into the abyss of history from which it was supposed to stand out and whose cyclical pattern it was meant to break means precisely the return of the repressed. What returns is the negativity of the state of nature: perhaps it is the "curse of humanity" which modernity sought to lift, perhaps it is the revenge of a dethroned God, or perhaps the return of Job (modern man ventured to live under this slogan too, "Never Again Job!"). The return of negativity is best visible in the fact that now only "negative events" take place, events which are destructive and which enhance chaos and disorder: the games in Sochi were not an event, the Annexation of Crimea was; the Occupy Movement, despite its presence, did not manage to transform into an event, but the financial crisis of 2008 and its aftershocks were an event, even if it was subcutaneous. However, the return of negativity takes place in slightly changed conditions—in the conditions of a tightening noose, both on the level of individuals and communities.

For this reason, the drive toward greatness cannot put on the modernist costume but it must somehow negotiate with the conditioning of turbo-capitalistic deregulation, flexibility, mobilization, intensification and leveling which take place within the conditions of social production of subjects. It cannot be stoically insensitive to these phenomena, especially since they touch the heart of the drive to greatness, squeezing it into tighter and tighter spaces and imposing a growing number of pressures, micro-coercions, little necessities, small fights, defenses and attacks as well as belt tightening (or austerity): all this multiplies discontinuities, re-adaptations and reterrito-rializations. In such conditions the drive toward greatness takes the form of increasingly fragmentary and niche processes—greatness is ground up under the pressure of growing population density and the devastation of the civilizational insurance against "natural coercion" which was once en-joyed without the worry that it may one day be cancelled due to "excess of people". Contrary to the ideology of the "danger of negative popula-tion growth"—always an ethnocentric argument since globally population growth has been positive—man multiplies too fast and population increase is no mark of success, against what is sometimes suggested by vulgar evolu-tion. This "too fast" is not an expression of Malthusian misanthropy; what is at stake here is mainly the psychological and social impact of population growth on the possibility of individual empowerment—it is again becoming a luxury, a less and less available good. In the context of the free market, individual becoming-subject is only possible at the level below elementary, mainly in our free time, and free time falls prey to drastic cuts and transfers to the privileged classes. Of course, the pressure is partly generated by the transfer of significant amounts of labour into quasi-slave economies: the de-emancipation of the West owes much of its power to the labour of Chinese, Indian, Pakistani, Thai or other workers. Although this transfer, at least in the beginning, brought about the illusion of new consumer prosperity in the West (cheap goods), it has ultimately led to massive disillusionment: the specter of unemployment undermines consumer satisfaction. It is, in a way, a setback for thought since it must now insist on ideas which in the 1970s and even in the 1990s could be thought of as standards forever achieved. Subjectivity returns, or better, thought returns to the notion of subjectivity precisely due to the fact that it has ceased to be something socially obvious and civilizationally given. There is a threat of a return of slavery and universal mass disempowerment which will certainly be nothing familiar but will once more enslave the majority, this time in an entirely new style, without shackles. It will most likely be a quiet and invisible slavery: slavery at a higher level. At the lower level, the material degeneration of the standard of living can assume quite real and tangible forms—this threat is already haunting the West.

As old ghosts return in new variants and realizations which occur in the previously unknown conditions of overpopulation and crisis as well as intensified exploitation of natural and human resources, there is no time to smell the roses. That is why the purely aesthetic drive towards greatness can bear some impatience in the audience. The audience needs discreet, delicate and unimposing action, something less entitled. Excessively loud egocentrism has become somewhat shameful and almost anachronistic as modern man dwindles and fails as a grand project: this is not a world for an individual man dressed in the glory of his singular splendor. Even individuality aimed at greatness must satisfy itself with the small greatness of "the weak", more masterless than "master" gestures and achievements. It must do without aristocratism, however lofty. Instead, it must embrace the fragility and hopelessness of one's condition—one's sickliness, powerlessness and futility.

The death of death is the last consequence of the "end of grand narratives". Incidentally, this very formula is evidently another form of grand narration and as such joins the familiar list of great philosophical paradoxical truths (perhaps the most beautiful truths of all) which cancel themselves out yet manage to show a problem—they are not empty. As is well known, grand narratives accompanied the Enlightenment projects of emancipation, progress and the moral development of man, and the fact that they have been decomposed as great secular Teleologies and Theodicies of post-Christian modernity does not mean that any new perspective has thereby been opened: the end of grand narratives, the end of ends, is in fact the end of beginnings, the end of the conception of beginning as the possibility of a new opening, a new hand, a significant reconfiguration of the system. This is why the 21st century is the time of great apprehensions rather than great expectations. The Enlightenment faith in the "better tomorrow" and its unfinished emancipatory civilizational project (which, as an enterprise of the capitalist machine may have been, from the very beginning, a smokescreen for what in practice always was and still remains an increase of wealth and exploitation—this suspicion is an immortal and ever timely point of Marxism) have managed to lose so many battles that it might be time for it to finally lose the war: the 21st century announces itself with fanfare as the age of the worse tomorrow. The death of death does not carry any gospel. It is a time of black clouds and quiet panic—the savings bonds of rationalistic optimism are yielding less than ever before in the history of modernity, except perhaps the 1930s. They are junk bonds.

However, one can try to replace the grand teleological narratives with medium ones, ones which exclude talk of the final goal, end, progress and the rational plan of some kind of history, but which show its entirety as always a fragment of something indefinitely larger and infinite. These may be attempts at a synthetic presentation of great historical topoi such as "modernity" and the like thematic blocks, although without any imperialist historiosophic ambitions. One can also report on the now—this is another specific method of "self-knowledge", one which is always timely even if it is somehow abstractly "detached" (what is the now?). For some it may be intellectually attractive to entertain, precisely in reaction to "the eternal return of negativity", the nihilistic narration of the crawling catastrophe of which T.S. Eliot wrote: "This is the way the world ends. Not with a bang, but a whimper." To negate negativity is futile and at the same time inevitable (Ecclesiastics strikes back)—such is life in naked simplicity and immediate shamelessness, life utterly robbed of enlightenment where one can do no more and no less than delay the catastrophe and prolong the agony: persist. With a bit of goodwill, whose existence should not be denied to anyone *a priori*, not even to the postmodern man in his permanent state of bankruptcy, such nihilism can lead to what we may call affirmative nihilism.

Affirmative nihilism does not lead to the negation and ultimate humiliation of our daily sense but rather to the discovery of the deep though hopeless dimension of the opposition to nothingness. Is there anything particularly lofty and momentous about such an opposition? Not necessarily, but here it is. All we do, all our efforts, including those most burdensome and ungrateful, zero out in the face of futility and at the same time are inevitable to delay the end. Nothing good will come of them, there will be no plus other than the fact that owing to them things will get no worse—while stupidity, wickedness and hatred will always find enough pretext and hotbeds, and enough destructive power which leads into the abyss, enough supporters, agitators and money. All we do to render stupidity, wickedness and hatred somehow shyer and weaker, all we do to slow them down and lessen their impetus, is deeply valuable in terms of the protection of being from the inevitable. At the same time, due to an increase in overall mass, the overall "gravitational force", each single action is subject to inflation and the value of our efforts is continuously diminished.

This leads to the last observation regarding subjectivity in its current state, after the death of death and the end of grand emancipatory narratives, and at the same time at the moment when subjectivity turns out to be that which persistently returns. Despite the death of subjectivity, its deconstruction and decomposition, it still exists, it still lasts, although maltreated and broken. At the same time, its practice and social conditioning, its daily lot, transforms it more and more clearly into marginal subjectivity. Subjectivity returns in the movement of "de-emancipation": the "individual" has perhaps never in the modern world been as negligible, fragile, liable, replaceable and anonymous as he is now. This is not a world of individual men but a world of individualized exploitation of human resources and individually profiled self-knowledge understood as professional development. And this is the best case scenario, since outside of the minority stratum of professionals it is a world of intellectual invalids whose individualism is shaped by serial production. This world has long done without irreplaceable people, even if one can still find in it—perhaps more and more—outstanding individuals, although in most cases their greatness is entirely random.

However, the great ones are after all not as important as the average ones, those who somehow aspire—and the latter are subject to growing pressure, their subjectivity is exposed to the more and more brutal and tough conditions in the naked effort to survive. Their subjectivity is more and more doubtful and fragile, more and more "precarious". This is where our faith in the possibility of greatness converges with reality, with the "Real" whose deepest truth is negligibility, marginality, the fight for every scrap. This is why our faith in greatness must settle on certain minimalism and become absolutely modest and even ascetic, as it exists in circumstances which belittle and devalue individual actions, dissolving them in the flood of like actions: there are millions or at least thousands of people just like you. Each one demands something, each one is driven by his own ambitions and the competition is growing. The common aspiring of subjects is simultaneously the principle of the hyperinflation of their actions, gestures and achievements. The maintenance cost of subjectivity is increasing and the subsequent cuts, reductions and austerity measures weaken its security, releasing it back into the cold hands of nature—the return of cruelty and savagery à la Hobbes. The only original and unprecedented form of subjectivity generated by the current situation is perhaps the ultra-plutocratic subject of whom Peter Sloterdijk said in an interview from 2009: "Only the rich can save us" (probably a parody of the famous last words of Heidegger).[36] Because they have so much to lose, they must find some way out of the crisis. However, this is most likely merely a veiled and farcical appraisal of the misery of the human condition, expressed in line with the tradition of Aristippus of Cyrene so that the potentially mighty sponsors of the philosopher have the impression that someone intelligent flatters them, admires their industry and good intentions. Unfortunately for all of us, the truth is that their reason does not match their power and so the ultra-plutocratic caste and its quiet "drift toward oligarchy", as it has been recently dubbed by the political

36 Cited after: http://www.newsweek.pl/tylko-bogaci-moga-uratowac-swiat,43106, 1,1.html.

economist Thomas Picketty in the context of the current trends of global capitalism where the top one percent of the population controls 43 percent of wealth,[37] will lead to breakdown and an explosion more likely than to an easing of the growing tension whose short term yet orgiastically feverish beneficiary is that very caste. Sloterdijk simply wanted to wittily convey that nothing can save us anymore.

However, in the face of the marginality and fragility of the subject, other "average" and "small" narratives appear to be more important and are likely the broadest area of positive exploration and affirmative theory which remains available to us today. By regaining the emancipatory function at the micro level, such narratives give voice to that which is great in the small and marginal, to that which is heroic in the effort of transforming weakness into strength, in sensitivity and susceptibility to being hurt.

The ideal of the powerful autotelic and autonomic subject, subject-sovereign, is replaced by a different one: the humiliated and alienated subject who is far from the constitutive power of dominance, the non-master subject devoid of control and exposed to the extra-discursive experience of the fragility of the body, as is explored by Judith Butler in the context of the conditions of subjective being under the category of precariousness. Precariousness means being dependent, conditioned and subject to changing and unstable circumstances.[38] The other unmasks and compromises the ideal of subjective autonomy which assumes the individual as a subject of the law, a "sovereign" who can be threatened by that other. When that happens, the autonomous subject ventures to secure his rights at all cost, which leads to an extra-judicial eruption of violence against the one who, now construed as a threat to subjectivity, is no longer perceived as a subject. The other is turned into an "abject", an outcast or a bastard whose vulnerability is not equal to or even commensurable with the sensitivity and offence on the part of the subject-sovereign. As such, the other ceases to be an object of compassion and becomes an object of abuse: the cruelty of those allegedly more civilized. Those who "threaten our freedom" are barbarians who wear rags and filthy beards (such is at least our opinion) and live in primitive villages—this makes

---

37 Cited after *Gazeta Wyborcza* (*The Electoral Gazette*), 28 April 2014.
38 Compare, J. Butler, *Precarious Life*, Verso 2004.

them abject and turns them into morally and practically easy targets who deserve their lot, and even if they do not, they still constitute an inevitable cost in the war against evil. Given this, the proportion where significantly more "enemies" die for every one of "ours" seems natural and obvious. As Butler notes, consent for cruel means of warfare, inconsistent with the standards of democratic civilization (such as secret prisons, torture and drone attacks), is accompanied by the sense of victimhood and constant threat characteristic for the offended subject of the law.[39] Regardless of that opposition and the immense gap between the subject and the other whose suffering counts less because it is something "lesser" and illegal, it must be noted that the other's littleness is also our own, that his precariousness is no different than ours but that it is shared by all—what we all share is the fact that life is fragile.

In all this one can find the last dim spark of affirmation and "minor stabilization": if our life is defined by fragility and the delay of the inevitable end, and our decadent short-term and misty condition by the creeping unspoken bankruptcy of the Enlightenment project of "modern man", then we must forget about the great anthropological challenges of Nietzschean or super-humanist style and put them back where they have always belonged: in the sphere of myth and poetry. Instead, we should concentrate on the more realistic care for the preservation of some minimum of decency, and we should not go too far in pessimism regarding that minimum. A minimum of moral and material decency instead of the maximalization of genius and absolutization of individuality—this is perhaps what we should seek rather than continue to raise the bar for both the general and the private and intimate sphere. A minimum of decency is already a lot. It is enough, there is no greater duty. Moral and anthropological minimalism without oomph and fanfare, without exorbitant requirements and excessive expectations and ambitions, yet with an empathetic and tolerant attitude is ultimately fundamental. It is also something an individual can plausibly hold on to in these times of a worse tomorrow. We should at least not worsen the situation: *primum non nocere*. Not to be entitled towards being and other people, not to require of them less than of oneself, and of oneself not more than is assumed within basic decency and measure, without exaggeration, without

---

39 J. Butler, *Frames of War: When Life Is Grievable*, Verso 2009.

puffing up your chest to the point of ridiculousness and extremism. And most of all to understand that to force others to exert maximum effort and engage in the common pushing and shoving is a form of quiet aggression which needs to be eliminated—one does not have to do one's best, give it one's all. It is enough to give a little bit, anything really: one way or another, you are merely delaying the inevitable. You do not have to be overly eager and unrelenting, you do not have to be the pioneer of being, you do not have to flex your muscles to the point where they tear... loosen up, relax and breathe deep.

12. Selected Bibliography

Theodor W. Adorno, Max Horkheimer, *Dialectics of enlightenment*, Standord University Press 2002

Theodor W. Adorno, *Negative Dialectics*, Bloomsbury 2000

Hannah Arendt, *The Human Condition*, University of Chicago Press, 1958

Judith Butler, *Precarious Life. The Powers of Mourning and Violence*, Verso 2004

Judith Butler, *Frames of War. When is Life Grievable?*, Verso 2009

P.M. Churchland, *The Engine of Reason, the Seat of the Soul. A Philosophical Journey into the Brain*, The MIT Press 1996

Daniel Defoe, *Robinson Crusoe*, Penguin Books 1999

Gilles Deleuze, Felix Guattari, *What is Philosophy?*, Columbia University Press 1994

Michel Foucault, *Hermeneutics of the Subject*, Palgrave Macmillan 2005

G.W.F. Hegel, *Phenomenology of the Spirit*, Oxford University Press 1977

G.W.F. Hegel, *Philosophy of History*, Dover Publications 1956

Jean-Francois Lyotard, *The Postmodern Condition: A Report on Knowledge*, Manchester University Press 1984

Alasdair MacIntyre, *After Virtue*, University of Notre Dame Press 1984

Karl Marx, *The Economic and Philosophic Manuscripts of 1844*, Prometheus Books 1988

Marcus Aurelius, *Meditations*, Dover Publications 1997

Friedrich Nietzsche, *Ecce Homo*, Penguin Books 1992

Friedrich Nietzsche, *On the Genealogy of Morals*, Oxford University Press 1996

Friedrich Nietzsche, *The Birth of Tragedy: Out of the Spirit of Music*, Penguin Books 1994

Rüdiger Safranski, *Nietzsche: A Philosophical Biography*, Granta Books 2002

Peter Sloterdijk, *Critique of Cynical Reason*, University of Minnesota Press 1988

Peter Sloterdijk, *You must change your life*, Polity Press 2013

Peter Sloterdijk, *In the World Interior of Capital*, Polity Press 2013

Modernity in Question
Studies in Philosophy, Sociology and History of Ideas

Edited by Małgorzata Kowalska

www.peterlang.com

www.ingramcontent.com/pod-product-compliance
Lightning Source LLC
Chambersburg PA
CBHW031542260326
41914CB00002B/223